HUMAN GEOGRAPHY

HUMAN GEOGRAPHY

by

EMRYS JONES

Professor of Geography, London University

1972

CHATTO & WINDUS

LONDON

PUBLISHED BY
CHATTO AND WINDUS (EDUCATIONAL) LTD
42 WILLIAM IV STREET
LONDON W.C.2

*

CLARKE, IRWIN AND CO LTD
TORONTO

First Published 1964
Second Impression 1965
Third Impression 1965
Fourth Impression 1967
Fifth Impression 1969
Second Edition 1972

ISBN 0 7011 0712 X (Net)
ISBN 0 7010 0091 0 (Non-Net)

PRINTED IN GREAT BRITAIN BY
BUTLER AND TANNER LTD
FROME AND LONDON

PREFACE

The term *Human Geography* is deceivingly all-inclusive. At sixth-form level human geography is too often either what remains of systematic geography after taking out physical bases, or it loosely encompasses all the regional work. This vagueness is by no means an asset. In a way one of the attractions of physical geography is that it has a scientific framework and is capable of generalisations. This is not so in human geography; yet I think some kind of logical framework is essential. This brief introduction to the subject begins with man, his numbers and distribution, then breaks down mankind into various groups. Within these groups and their impact on the earth arise the raw materials the human geographer studies. They are also the bases of more specialised aspects, such as social geography, political geography and economic geography, but in themselves they form a cohesive whole, and I hope that this, at least, will be apparent in the text.

I would like to express my thanks to my colleagues, Professor T. H. Elkins, Mr. D. J. Sinclair and Dr. J. E. Martin, for reading parts of the text and making useful comments on them, and to Mrs. E. Wilson and Miss E. E. Woodhams, for drawing the maps.

NOTE ON SECOND EDITION

Wherever possible the figures in the text of this edition have been brought up to date, and some changes of greater substance have been made in the sections on population, towns and cities, and more particularly communications, a chapter which has been expanded. Reading material has been amended where necessary and supplemented by recent books. Measurements are given in both metric and non-metric units throughout.

CONTENTS

MAPS AND DIAGRAMS

ACKNOWLEDGEMENTS

The author and publishers would like to thank the following for granting permission to use copyright material for illustrations:

The American Geographical Society for Fig. 9.5 from *The Geographical Review* and Fig. 3.4(*c*) from *Atlas of the Historical Geography of the United States*; John Bartholomew & Son Ltd. for Fig. 10.9 based on *The Times Atlas of the World*; Jonathan Cape Ltd. for Fig. 3.1 from *The History of Mankind* by Carleton S. Coon; T. W. Freeman and Methuen & Co. Ltd. for Fig. 10.7 based on a map from *Ireland* (1950); the Controller, H.M. Stationery Office, for Figs. 6.6, 6.8, 7.2, 9.3 and 10.4 based on Ordnance Survey Maps; the Chief Survey Officer of the Government of Northern Ireland for Figs. 6.10(*c*) and 10.3 based on Ordnance Survey maps of Northern Ireland; Oxford University Press for Figs. 9.8 and 9.9 from *A Social Geography of Belfast* by Emrys Jones; Penguin Books for Fig. 6.10 from *The Anatomy of the Village* by Thomas Sharp; Presses Universitaire de France for Fig. 2.4 from *Introduction à l'étude géographique de la population du monde* by Pierre George; The Town Planning Review and A. Sharon for Fig. 6.11 from 'Collective Settlements in Israel', *Town Planning Review*, Vol. 25, No. 4; Chatto & Windus Ltd. for 6.5(*a*), 6.5(*b*), and 10.6 from *Germany* by T. H. Elkins; and Pan American World Airways for the photograph of New York that appears on the cover.

Chapter 1

INTRODUCTION

Perhaps the first thing which one looks for in any book which
tries to introduce a specialised branch of knowledge is a definition of the subject and its relationship with wider fields of
knowledge. What is human geography, and where does it fit
into geography as a whole? Too brief an answer to the first
question could be misleading, as generalisations usually are; it
is hoped that the book itself is the answer if it will show those
aspects of human life which, through a continual and changing
interaction with nature in all its forms, have given rise to distinctive landscapes and regions. The second question calls for
a brief consideration of the entire field of geography.

Geographical thought has a very long history. It began when
men first interested themselves in the world in which they
lived and speculated on man's place in it. Some concerned
themselves with describing this world, its natural phenomena
and its people and their ways; these were the so-called topo-
graphical writers, who, from the Greeks down to the present
day, have contributed so much to our store of factual knowledge. Others were more scientific, analytic and speculative.
These measured the earth, they generalised on its features, they
put it in its setting of the universe: these were the cosmo-
graphers, whose curiosity extended to the whole cosmos. Only
some of these early thinkers called themselves geographers:
Strabo, for example, and Ptolemy, both of whom made massive
contributions which were unequalled in their scope for many
centuries. But in Greek and Roman times more inclusive and
less specialised – indeed hardly differentiated – geographical information was culled and passed on by many thinkers to whom
the word 'geography' might have meant nothing. Herodotus'
writing is full of such information: Greek philosophers and
mathematicians made a great contribution, much of which was

preserved by Arab scholars, to find its way back into Europe in post-medieval times and be a part of the renaissance of learning. Although geographers have drawn greatly on such work it can rarely be called specifically geographical, for there was no conscious attempt at a discipline with its own aims, its own methods, its own mode of thought. Such thinking is relatively recent. Modern geography emerged in the 19th century from the previous vaguer undifferentiated knowledge, first by systematising our knowledge of areal phenomena and secondly by showing their inter-relatedness. Systematisation is still apparent in the way in which people usually plan regional descriptions, beginning with geology and relief, going on to climate, soils, vegetation, and then introducing human society, past and present. The inter-relatedness of these phenomena has often been expressed as the way in which the physical environment affected man, i.e. as environmental determinism. Man has always been conscious of his environment, and particularly of the forces in that environment over which he has so little control, which often seem to control him. In the past he has thought of these forces as extending beyond his immediate environment to the sun, moon and stars. (Very many people still read, and half believe, forecasts of their behaviour in daily or weekly horoscopes.) Small wonder that men thought of society as being moulded by these natural forces: that Ritter could talk of the influence of mountains on man, for example, and of man as being incapable of escaping nature's processes. The ideas which pictured man as a pawn moved to the dictates of so-called natural laws fitted well into 19th-century scientific thought. This was one of the main theses of Freidrich Ratzel (1844–1904) who, in the last decade of the 19th century, laid the foundations of human geography as we know it today and gave it a position and standing on a par with physical geography.

To emphasise the place of man in his geography, Ratzel called his first great work *Anthropogeography*. It appeared in two volumes in 1882 and 1891. It was followed later by a *History of Mankind* and *Political Geography*. In this way Ratzel stressed that the approach to geography should be made through man, and that this was as fundamental as the analysis which physical geographers were making of the natural environment. The emphasis was one which was broadened and developed particularly in France in the first half of this century. During this period it is to France that we turn, not only for outstanding regional monographs with their ordered analyses of a wealth of information, or for the great *Géographie Universelle*, but also for landmarks in the systematisation of human geography contained in the works of Vidal de la Blache, J. Brunhes, A. Demangeon and others. Vidal de la Blache (1845–1918) perhaps had the greatest breadth of interests, for his studies draw upon a vast range of anthropology and history, human data which he deemed necessary to explain the peculiarities of the geography of man. Brunhes's vision was more restricted, his aim more limited; although he attempted a classification and systematisation of the subject he rarely went farther than the present-day landscape as he saw it. Perhaps the best of both has been brought into the works of Max Sorre, whose three great volumes on the *Foundations of Human Geography* is more systematised than de la Blache while retaining something of his breadth of vision, whereas it has more depth than Brunhes: it is an attempt at a complete human geography, social, economic and political.

Although the human geography which the French school explored so thoroughly owed its origin largely to Ratzel, there was one fundamental aspect of the latter's work against which they reacted very sharply. Ratzel was an out-and-out environmental determinist. The extreme of this view can be summed up in his own words: 'Man must live on the land nature has given him . . . submitting to the law.' 'Must', 'submitting' and 'law' echo familiar scientific attitudes in 19th-century biology. The task of the geographer, according to Ratzel, was to study *how* the environment affected man. The French school tried to place the relationship between man and his environment on a new basis. This is why Vidal de la Blache so emphasised man's culture and history, and why, later, H. J. Fleure was to state that geography, anthropology and history were a trilogy which you could not break without great loss. Vidal de la Blache did not shift the aim of geography to a study of man–he was quite adamant that geography is a study of 'place'—but he affirmed man's part in making 'place' what it was, and implicitly denied that the environment was always compulsive. This feeling, shared by other geographers of that school, that man had a positive part to play and that he must be able to exercise his will, was best expressed by another Frenchman, Lucien Febvre, who in his book *Geographical Introduction to History* put it succinctly by stating: 'There are nowhere necessities, but everywhere possibilities.' He looked upon the environment as presenting man with a number of possibilities from which he could choose his own course of action. 'Possibilism' became—and still is to many—an acceptable basis for discussing the relationship between man and environment. It does allow the significance of cultural and historical factors to be taken into account: it allows man to be a decision maker, though still within a framework which is limiting and partly restrictive.

During the last decade interest has focused on a new departure in human geography—locational analysis, summarised in a recent book by Haggett. The complexities of numerous relationships are simplified in order to understand the fundamental processes. Regularities are sought in the way activities are manifest on the earth's surface. The geographer discovers these regularities and expresses them mathematically or as models. The results do not necessarily supplant the kinds of explanations discussed above, but locational analysis does present a new way of looking at the problem. It adds a dimension to geography which is enriching the subject and suggesting exciting new departures.

It needs very little reflection to realise that in methodological discussions one is often forced to simplify. 'Man and the land', 'man and environment' are phrases which we use glibly, forgetting that they signify very complex ideas. 'Man' is an abstraction. In the first part of this book it will be stressed that we are not dealing with 'man', but with men: men of different colour, language, creed, society, organisation and history: this was what Vidal de la Blache saw so clearly. 'Environment' is equally complex. It would be comforting to be able to think of environment as a given, so-called 'natural', entity, into which men came when beckoned by the geographer so that he could assess the interactions more easily. But human geography is not a study of Adam in a Garden of Eden. We are faced not only with an immensely diversified society, but with an environment much of which has long since ceased to be 'natural', which bears the heavy imprint of man. Indeed we are forced to realise the truth that the two components are often *one*, that it is the geographer who has separated them, and that perhaps he is creating an artificial world of his own to satisfy his speculations. No one can deny man's ability to change much of the landscape. How much 'natural' environment do we see in south-east England for example? We see fields and hedgerows and ditches, roads and fences, houses and gardens, the cumulative effect of centuries of use. If we live in a city we are even more likely to be conscious only of streets, office blocks and light standards. We spend much of our time in an artificial climate in heated buildings, with artificial lighting: this is our environment. In other words the relationships which the human geographer tries to analyse are often between particular groups of men and a man-made environment: and the latter has been the outcome of other relationships between different groups of men and a less transformed environment. It is important to view these relationships with all the historical depth that they imply.

The words 'relationship' and 'interaction' have been used frequently in the last few pages. These arise from the processes of human geography, and although they are of particular interest to some geographers, they are complementary only to the study of 'place', to an analysis of what arises from these processes. This leads us back to the concept of the whole, to the geographical situation which the geographer tries to study. Some geographers are afraid that too much stress has been laid on the separate identity of the two main elements in the process, society and physical environment, to the detriment of the study as a whole. Over-specialisation in the past may have tended towards an underestimation of the unity of the subject; but whatever one may think of the methodological arguments for or against the so-called 'duality' which the above discussion introduced, there is no gainsaying its usefulness in the organisation of the subject. Organisation demands classification, however artificial some of the dividing lines prove to be, and it is still convenient to talk of physical geography, biogeography and human geography. The last covers several fields of study: historical, population, settlement, urban, political and medical geography, and the geography of resources, economic and agricultural geography, minerals and manufacturing and transport. Within human geography these specialised topics will continue to multiply as new problems stimulate new interests and as they become defined by geographers working in those fields. But all we are doing is putting our knowledge into convenient pigeon-holes. Whatever philosophical stand one may take about which of these elements is uppermost, which has the greater effect on the final outcome, these need not blind us to the unity of the whole nor impede our efforts at analysing and describing both the world in which we live and the way in which we live in that world.

SUGGESTIONS FOR FURTHER READING

P. AMBROSE: *Analytical Human Geography* (Longman), 1969.

P. VIDAL DE LA BLACHE: *Principles of Human Geography* (Constable), 1959.

G. R. CRONE: *Modern Geographers* (Royal Geographical Society), 1951.

L. FEBVRE: *A Geographical Introduction to History* (Routledge), 1950.

P. HAGGETT: *Locational Analysis in Human Geography* (Arnold), 1965.

J. H. G. LEBON: *An Introduction to Human Geography* (Hutchinson), 1961.

S. W. WOOLDRIDGE and W. G. EAST: *The Spirit and Purpose of Geography* (Hutchinson), 1960.

Among texts which cover the whole field of human geography are:

J. O. N. BROCK and J. W. WEBB: *Geography of Mankind* (McGraw-Hill), 1968.

P. E. JAMES and H. V. B. KLINE: *A Geography of Man* (Ginn), Boston, 1959.

Ed. W. L. THOMAS: *Man's Role in Changing the Face of the Earth* (University of Chicago Press), 1956.

P. L. WAGNER and M. W. MIKESELL: *Readings in Cultural Geography* (University of Chicago Press), 1962.

Chapter 2

POPULATION

2.1 WORLD POPULATION AND ITS GROWTH

The most fundamental element of human geography is man himself, and the first questions which a human geographer must ask are: what is the number of mankind, its distribution on the surface of the earth, its density, and why are there so many inequalities of distribution and density? Although the answers to many of these questions lie in cultural differences between various societies of men, we can begin by regarding man as more or less the same the world over and consider first his numbers and distribution.

The total population of the world in 1969 was approximately 3,520 million. To appreciate this we must realise how quickly the numbers are changing, how recent have been the great increases and what even greater increases we may expect in the near future. It has been estimated that the population of the world in 1850 was about 1,200 million, so that the growth in the last hundred years or so has been greater than that in the entire previous history of mankind – which may be 100,000 years or considerably more. The population may well double in another generation.

Estimates of world population in the early history of mankind must necessarily be guesses: but at the beginning of the food-producing revolution, when settled agricultural communities began to replace bands of hunters and gatherers, perhaps about 6000 B.C., world population was unlikely to be less than 1 million or more than 5 million. The advances of agriculture which laid the basis of the riverine civilisations heralded great increases in numbers, possibly as much as 250 million by the beginning of the Christian era – i.e. an increase of between 6 per cent and 10 per cent a century. Estimates of world population in 1650, prior to the agrarian and industrial revolutions in Europe, vary from 470 million to 545 million, making the preceding increase between 2½ per cent and 5 per cent a century. But in the last three hundred years the increase has been 65 per cent a century, and in the last hundred years, over 100 per cent. The upward sweep of the population graph is very striking (Fig. 2.1).

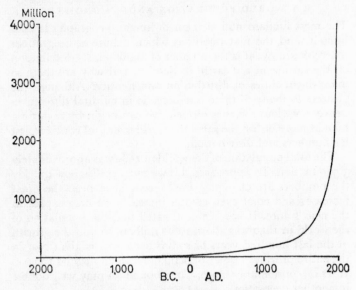

Fig. 2.1. Increase in world population.

Opinions differ greatly in estimating future growth, but they all indicate a very marked increase. It is rather disconcerting that the estimates of future world population themselves increase so much as the data on which they are based become more reliable. Previous estimates are always proved to have been too conservative. U.N.O. have made three estimates for 1980, which are shown at the top of the opposite page.

It is safe to assume that by 1980 the population of the world will be at least 4,000 million, and by A.D. 2000 it will probably be between 6,000 million and 7,000 million.

Year of estimate	Million		Million	Mid-value
1951	Between 2,976	and	3,636	3,306
1954	,, 3,295	,,	3,990	3,643
1958	,, 3,850	,,	4,280	4,065

Not all parts of the world share equally in this rapid rise. Nor of course is our knowledge of all parts equally detailed: the percentage error is probably about 5·0 per cent in Africa and Asia – and may indeed be 10 per cent in eastern Asia – but in Europe and North America 0·5 per cent is normal, and 2 per cent is usual in South America. Even allowing for this, the differences in population changes in recent years can be gauged quite easily from the following table.

Area	Population millions, 1966	Percentage increase per annum, 1960–1966	Birth rate per 1,000	Death rate per 1,000	Area, square kilometres (000s)	Population density per square kilometre
World	3,356	1·9	34	16	135,697	25
Africa	318	2·3	46	23	30,244	11
America	470	2·2	32	11	42,068	11
North	217	1·5	22	9	21,515	10
Latin	253	2·8	41	13	20,553	12
Asia	1,868	2·0	38	18	27,543	68
East	864	1·4	33	19	11,755	73
South	1,004	2·5	43	18	15,788	64
Europe	449	0·9	18	10	4,929	91
Oceania	18	2·1	26	11	8,511	2
U.S.S.R.	233	1·4	22	7	22,402	10

(U.N. Demographic Year Book, 1966.)

The percentage increase of world population 1960–6 was 1·9 a year; Africa, Latin America and South Asia had a considerably greater increase than average. Europe was well below average, and so were North America, East Asia and the

U.S.S.R. The comparatively small differences in percentage increase should, however, be related to absolute numbers in each region. A 2·3 per cent increase in Africa relates to a population of 318 million, whereas a 2 per cent increase in Asia relates to 1,868 million. In other words, between 1960 and 1966 Africa's population increased by about 4 million, Asia's by 208 million with constant rates of increase, in 1976 there will be 80 million more Africans in the world and 403 million more Asians than in 1966. In the same decade, Europeans will increase by only 40 million. Growth will be most conspicuous in Latin America, where 253 million will increase by 77 million. The significance of this is not simply that the proportions of these peoples will alter, because this would be comparatively slight, as the table below shows. But it does mean

Area	Population 1966 (millions)	Percentage of world population	Projected population, 1976	Percentage of world population	Increase, 1966–76 (millions)
World	3,356	100·00	4,047	100·00	691
Africa	318	9·48	398	9·84	80
Asia	1,868	55·96	2,271	56·11	403
Europe	449	13·38	489	12·08	40
Latin America	253	7·54	330	8·15	77

that a disproportionately greater number of persons will be added to the population in the very regions where pressure is now greatest and where problems of over-population are most acute, i.e. in south-west Asia, India and Latin America. Before discussing further the reasons for these changes we should look in more detail at the distribution of world population.

2.2 POPULATION DISTRIBUTION

The striking feature of the distribution of mankind on the earth's surface is its apparent haphazard nature (Fig. 2.2). It

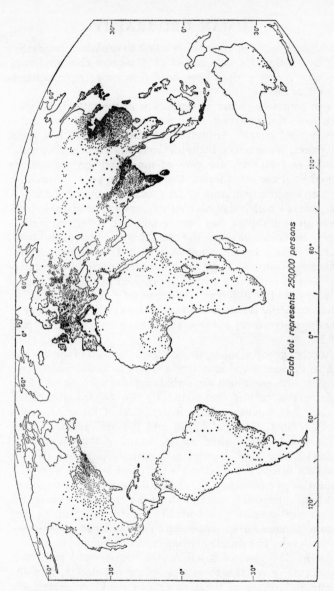

Each dot represents 250,000 persons

Fig. 2.2. Distribution of world population.

has always been the geographer's task to explain it rationally: this is usually done in terms of physical and climatic limits, though it is easy to show how insufficient such simple explanations may be.

The empty lands are as significant as the settled, for most men have shunned vast areas because of their unfavourable climate and terrain. Around the Arctic Sea there is a great peripheral waste which includes Greenland, much of Canada, Alaska and Siberia, a region of snow and ice and tundra ringed by dense taiga forest land. Man can get to terms with such an environment only under special conditions of adaptation, one of which is that his distribution must be sparse indeed. Such an equilibrium has been established – often very effectively – by simple societies, like the Eskimo. Much of this land, then, seems empty but is not uninhabited. With hunting and gathering economies there are great areas north of the apparent limit of settlement which are utilised at simple stages of economy. Using different techniques of adaptation even an urban economy is now being pushed far north, particularly in Siberia, where there are several large towns between 70° and 75° N.

Another group of inhospitable regions consists of the hot and temperate deserts and scrublands, where lack of moisture often coupled with great heat are forbidding obstacles. North of the equator this belt is dominated by the Sahara and Saudi Arabia; but almost as difficult are parts of Inner Mongolia (Gobi), Tibet, the Aral basin, and the arid regions of the south-west of the United States. South of the equator the Kalahari, vast areas of west and central Australia, and the Atacama desert, are relatively uninhabited. Again there is a certain degree of transition. Oases, the use of artesian water, and man's determination to extract minerals, however severe the physical conditions, all modify the simple statement that certain climates forbid settlement. The challenge is again met on two levels. The simple herding economy, such as that of the Badawin (Bedouin) of Saudi Arabia, interspersed with oasis agriculture, gives rise to only a sparse population, and the simple techniques of these economies could never entirely overcome difficulties such as absolute lack of water: within such an absolute limit, the Badawin utilise even desert lands. The second level depends on the advance of Western technology, which can overcome so many difficulties if economically justified, and to which, theoretically, there seem to be limitless possibilities.

A third region which has proved difficult to man is the zone of tropical rain forest, where nature, no longer stinting, chokes with an abundance of life. Amazonia and parts of south-east Asia are conspicuous examples. Gatherers, at the simplest level of culture, have for centuries past thinly peopled this area; and the extremes of heat and moisture have failed to keep out the metal or oil prospector. In parts of central America even civilisation has once flourished, then withdrawn, and its relics have again been choked by vegetation.

Lastly, there are empty areas scattered over the distribution map which reveal man's difficulties in conquering altitude. The physiological obstacles to living at great heights are considerable, and few areas over 3000 m/10,000 ft are settled. The exceptions are notable, showing not only that man will achieve the exceptional for economic gain, but that he can adapt himself remarkably to flourishing urban life at these altitudes, as in the Andean cities of La Paz (3,630 m/11,909 ft), Sucre (2,830 m/9,300 ft) and Quito (2,850 m/9,350 ft).

The simple picture of empty lands, with its suggestion of definite limits to man's activities, must, therefore, be modified by several considerations. Some simple societies do exist in some of these lands, many showing the most subtle adaptations to very difficult climatic conditions. It is possible that this extremely thin cover of human beings is a relict of what conditions were once over the most of the earth's surface. The so-called 'settled areas' are in fact a further stage in man's history at which density was considerably increased. Another consideration is the degree to which Western civilisation, with its very advanced techniques, is breaking into these empty lands, sometimes transitorily in search of metals, sometimes more permanently with new means of adaptation. Arising from these it should be remembered that limits are flexible; both absolute limits and the vague border-line between settled and apparent void are fluctuating constantly. Some would argue that these fluctuations are small, that man has reached the effective limit of settlement, and that major changes in the world pattern are unlikely. But when one considers recent changes in Siberia, for example, it is not unreasonable to suppose that the exploitation of the northern zones sometime in the future may make the Canadian settlement limit of today appear no more than a temporary halt to movement northwards.

Looking again at the distribution map it is obvious that in some regions man has prospered. The abundance of moisture and the richness of life in monsoon lands, where conditions so often allow double cropping, is the background of a vast concentration of people. But it is man's ability to regulate water by irrigation methods which has led to this concentration, and its distribution is limited less by climate than by the spread of traditional methods of farming. Similarly, conditions in Europe were such that an abundance of food could be assured under certain conditions of cultivation and domestication; though again we must remember that cultivation and domestication first arose outside Europe. Vidal de la Blache sums it up by saying: 'The European agglomeration appears to be an achievement of intelligence and method as much as a natural phenomenon.' The North American concentration of people, smaller and much newer, adjusts itself to nature in much the same way as that of Europe: it is in fact an extension of the latter.

Is it profitable to try and relate this pattern in detail to the physical environment? I think not. However much those heavily populated belts may seem to be correlated with climatic zones, these zones serve no more than a descriptive use unless we assume (a) that there are definite limits to the belts of dense population, and (b) that there is a strong causal relationship between climate and human activity. In the final analysis the second assumption rests an opinion on how far man can adapt himself to varying climatic conditions, physiologically or by technical means. But in relating climate and population nothing is more striking than the anomalies. Similar environments do not have similar population patterns. Important though the physical and climatic background is, it is never a sufficient explanation of the distribution of mankind. The first assumption brings us to the arguments which suggested themselves over the absolute limit of human distribution. To relate causally the limits of dense population to climatic data is to suggest that the population pattern has reached a final stage. But this distribution is the latest in a series of stages, none of which could have been final, but each of which reflected a certain level of achievement. For example the distribution of population in Britain before the industrial revolution was vastly different from the distribution of today. World distribution of population, although in its completely negative areas reflecting man's difficulties in overcoming climatic and biological obstacles, should be related to man's stage of development.

World population distribution is dynamic. If man seems to have reached any limits, they are often the limits of his culture and technology rather than those of nature. In the past fundamental advances have upset and changed the distribution radically. Only in some regions and for some periods has there been a seeming equilibrium. The north-western European and North American concentrations of today reflect the technical advance of the industrial revolution. Other changes of this magnitude are not only possible but probable, and once again part of the world pattern of population may disintegrate and another slowly take its place.

2.3 POPULATION DENSITY

The variations in the map of distribution of population suggest great differences in density in various parts of the world. Density, which expresses population in terms of unit area, is a useful concept. But in its simplest form, as in the table on page 21, it gives too generalised a picture. World density is 25 persons per square kilometre, but this figure obviously means very little because man is so unevenly distributed, and it does not take into account basic differences between virtually uninhabited lands and densely populated lands. For the world regions as defined by U.N.O. the density varies from 2 persons per square kilometre in Oceania to 147 in Southern Europe. Europe and Monsoon Asia have the highest densities. Again these figures can be dealt with only as very broad generalisations: Oceania, for example, includes in its area the whole of Australia, so much of which is virtually empty, thus giving a very false impression of the settled areas of Oceania. Nor do these figures give us any idea of pressure on the land and possible overcrowding. However high the density figures for Britain, no one would suggest that conditions here are comparable with those in Monsoon Asia, although generalised figures may suggest it.

There are ways of overcoming the inadequacy of the generalised figure and the non-comparability of the figures–at least to some degree. One could, for example, use a ratio of persons per square kilometre of cultivated land. This is logical in that ultimately people depend on food, and agricultural societies ignore land which cannot be used for food production. Double-cropping introduces a complication, for in some monsoon lands the food produced represents twice the area of cropped land. Further complications arise simply because, under modern conditions of trade and exchange, the ratio of persons to agricultural land in Britain is neither meaningful nor comparable with an agricultural community elsewhere. The most refined index in use in agricultural communities is the number of agriculturally employed males per square kilometre.

Obviously we must invest the idea of density with something more meaningful than the generalisations we are apt to use. It has already been said that a dense population in Britain means something very different from a dense population in rural India. One would hesitate to say that Britain was grossly over-populated–in spite of the apparent congestion–for it is still absorbing an increasing population and at the same time maintaining its level of existence. Rural areas of India with similar densities may well be grossly over-populated and face acute problems of shortage and want as their population increases. Dense population is not necessarily over-population: nor does sparse always mean under-populated. According to Unstead 'over-population truly exists whenever a reduction in the number of people would enable a smaller population to earn a better living'. Famine and migration are two symptoms of over-population. To balance population and food resources where the latter have reached their limit, there has to be a death for every birth if migration is impossible, and even infanticide may be added to famine and disease. If the death rate is higher than the birth rate through lack of food it means that the population has outrun its means of support. Under-population, says Unstead, exists where the inhabitants of a country are so few that they cannot develop their resources effectively enough to better their conditions of life. This, he states, is found in the early stages of the development of a new country: the first settlers are content on a very meagre level of subsistence until immigration has enabled resources to be used so that a high level of existence is attained. Some would argue that there is such a thing as an optimum population, that is, the number of people most consistent with the greatest economic welfare. This is bound to be a varying number of people, depending on the level of existence which they achieve.

All these concepts should be used very carefully. Over-population is an obvious fact, both to observers and to populations who suffer from it. Famine and migration show how fine is the balance between man and the land, and how easily upset. The idea of under-population may involve something quite different, because it is usually judged so by Western values and standards irrespective of native cultures. Western Europeans settling in a 'new land'–and it is 'new' to the Europeans only, of course–exploit a different range of resources, and on a different level, from the indigenous people. In other words the native population may be at its optimum population, but the country may at the same time be deemed under-populated from the point of view of an incoming people with different technical equipment and a different set of values. This is not an argument for unquestioningly accepting the status quo. No one can ignore famines in India or

c

China – or even the bare subsistence level which is the alternative: nor must resources in sparsely populated countries necessarily be ignored because the indigenous people cannot exploit them themselves. But we should be aware that our criteria of over-population, under-population or optimum population, relate to our own standards; and we should be prepared to examine and respect values to which alien standards may be tied.

2.4 NATURAL INCREASE

Changes in numbers of people are brought about in two ways: natural increase, i.e. the difference between the birth rate and the death rate, and the movement or migration of people. The world total, obviously, is not affected by the latter, but regional figures often are, and migration is important enough to warrant a separate chapter. Here something must be said about natural increase, for although a full treatment of this subject is primarily of interest to a demographer, the human geographer should not be ignorant of the basic factors controlling the numbers of people.

The table on page 21 shows that the *birth rate* varies considerably. There are four regions with low birth rates, Europe (18 per 1,000), North America (22 per 1,000), Oceania (26 per 1,000) and U.S.S.R. (22 per 1,000); they are much lower than the rest of the world which has birth rates between 33 and 46. These figures do not mean very much unless taken in conjunction with *death rates*. These are low in those same regions which have low birth rates, 9 per 1,000 in North America, 10 per 1,000 in Europe, 11 per 1,000 in Oceania and 7 per 1,000 in U.S.S.R. The death rate is highest in Africa, and South Central and South East Asia. It has been established that increases in population are not so much the result of an increasing birth rate, but due mainly to a declining death rate. This latter trend has been uppermost in Europe and North America since 1850, and is now beginning to affect the rest of the world: today it is the main factor in population increases in Latin America, Asia and Africa.

Is this happening in the 3rd World.

In the latter half of the 19th century the death rate in north-west Europe was falling due to the opening up of new lands elsewhere, more and better food and a general improvement in production, coupled with better means of communication and distribution, stability of governments and better maintenance of law and order. What would now be called the standard of living went up greatly, playing a more important part than the control of disease, which was still in its first halting stages. These same conditions are thought to lead eventually to a declining birth rate, but whereas the effect on the death rate is immediate that on the birth rate is delayed. Since 1900 medicine has played an ever-increasing role in the diminishing death rate. In this half century infantile mortality has been dramatically reduced to such low figures as 19·6 per 1,000 in the United Kingdom, 14·4 per 1,000 in the Netherlands, 16·9 per 1,000 in Iceland and 23·4 per 1,000 in the United States. In Europe the highest figure is still as high as 71·5 per 1,000 in Yugoslavia, but even this is small compared with Brazil (170 per 1,000), India (146 per 1,000), Uganda (160 per 1,000). (Figures refer to 1959–61.) Although a decreasing infantile mortality is the most dramatic change in population control brought about by medicine, it has considerably affected death rates at all ages by controlling such diseases as plague, cholera, typhus, diphtheria and so on. The effect which medical science can have by controlling one disease was shown in Ceylon: in five years, between 1945 and 1950, its death rate diminished from 21 per 1,000 to 12 per 1,000, almost entirely due to the control of malaria.

In many countries such as the United Kingdom, United States and Norway, expectation of life at birth is now around the traditional three score years and ten: but it is still low in new countries like Brazil (39·25) and in most of Asia (India, for example, is 41·89 for men), where the exception is Israel (70·52 for men and 73·19 for women) with its Western European urban standards of living. Expectation of life in some European countries has only recently reached 60 (e.g. Portugal). In most of these countries with a low expectation, the perils of life are nearly always in the early years: in India the expectation of life at 70 is 8·07 for men, compared with 10·4 in the United States and 9·15 in the United Kingdom.

Increased expectation of life due to a falling death rate in one way leads to a higher birth rate, for women then have a much better chance of living through their years of fertility and producing more children. Fertility is the most critical factor in assessing increases. Birth rate is not a very refined index; crude birth rate is merely the number of live births per 1,000 population per annum. *Fertility rate* gives the number of live births annually per 1,000 women between the ages of 15 and 49. Of greater value still in showing if a population is replacing itself is the *gross reproduction rate*–i.e. the number of girls (potential mothers) born per 1,000 women between the ages of 15 and 49. Even this assumes that all women will survive the age of 49, so we can refine it still further to the *net reproduction rate*, where correction is made for mortality in the new generation. An example will make the last clearer. In Australia, between 1920 and 1922, each 1,000 women gave birth to 1,517 girl children. The gross reproduction ratio is: 1,517/1,000 = 1·517. Not all of those children, however, survived. Mortality tables showed that 1,318 would survive child-bearing age, so the net reproduction ratio is: 1,318/1,000 = 1·318. This means the population was more than replacing itself, other things being equal. A ratio of 1 shows replacement, a stable population if the death rate does not vary. For a time between the two world wars many European countries had a ratio less than 1. In England and Wales it fell below 1 for the first time in 1924, when it was 0·967, and it was as low as 0·773 in 1938. It reached 1·021 in 1944, fell a little in 1945, then rose to 1·03 in 1953. Sweden in 1926 fell to 0·971 and recovered to 1·06 in 1943. Sharing in the fall, Switzerland and Denmark both recovered in 1942. The United States, which fell below 1 in 1933, rose to 1·519 by 1953. In most Asian countries the ratio has been consistently above 1, and in some countries it is rapidly rising. In Ceylon in 1920-2 it was 1·16, in 1946 1·442 and in 1952 it was 1·987.

Discounting the post-war increases in net reproduction rates, in Europe and North America the dominant trend of the first half of this century was a decreasing birth rate, which affected population trends greatly. For example, in England and Wales the birth rate between 1900 and 1910 was 27·2 per 1,000 compared with 35·4 per 1,000 in 1871–80. This had dropped further to 16·7 in 1948–50. This trend has been general in Western Europe, North America and Australasia. In these regions this trend has been most marked among the so-called middle classes, where a conscious adjustment has been made to the increasing level of living. That is, the level of living can only be increased or maintained by decreasing the family voluntarily. The result has been a stationary population until the trends of the last fifteen years have shown a tendency to increase the size of the family.

Thinking in terms of world population, the most important step which is still to come, foreshadowed in the example above from Ceylon, is the dramatic lowering of the death rate in Asia, Africa and Latin America. The probable effects will be a staggering rise in population before any kind of equilibrium can be established or trends towards lowering the birth rate can begin. An increase comparable to that in Europe in the 19th century in the remainder of the old world–and so much greater in absolute numbers–would make even the most liberal estimates of increases appear small.

2.5 POPULATION STRUCTURE

So far we have dealt with population as if it were made up of equal units. This is appropriate in discussing distribution or growth, but to search a little deeper into the inter-relationships of society, economy and the land, then we must recognise that the structure of population varies greatly in different societies. For the moment it will suffice to see what follows from analysing population by age and sex. Society is made up of men and women, children, working people, and the aged who are so often dependent on others. In different societies the proportions in these classes vary, and this affects the life of all members of the society.

The simple sex ratios are not of great significance because they rarely depart radically from equality. In England and

Wales rather more boys than girls are born, but this ratio changes gradually as the percentage of women increases in the older age groups. Much more important is the division of society into age groups. This is usually shown by an age–sex pyramid (Fig. 2.3). In one kind of pyramid the number of males and females are recorded as bars in each five-year age group from o to 80+: this pyramid is useful also in giving the male/female ratio in each group. But pyramids of numbers of

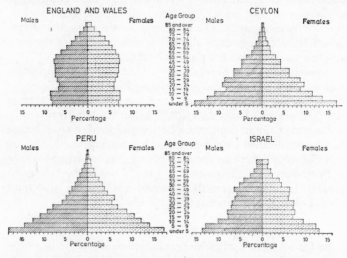

Fig. 2.3. Types of population structure shown by age/sex pyramids.

persons are impossible to compare, so the more usual pyramid shows the percentage males in each group on one side and the percentage females on the other. This simple diagram enables us to see at a glance what proportion of the population lies in each age group, and the shape of the pyramid immediately suggests the type of society portrayed. Assuming the hypothetical shape to be a pyramid–and the world figures closely approach this–then the age–sex pyramid for Ceylon is conspicuous for its broad base and the rapid tapering at the narrow peak. This pyramid is typical of many peasant communities in which there is a large number of children and in which a comparatively high death rate among older persons as well as children tapers off the older groups. Peru provides us with a more exaggerated example, with an enormous base and very rapid tapering, for here 55·7 per cent of the males and 54·3 per cent of the females are under 20, and only 4·3 per cent and 5·1 per cent respectively are over 60. In great contrast to this is the pyramid for England and Wales, fairly typical of an advanced industrial community. Here the base is contracted, and would be more so if it were not for the post-war increase in the birth rate: the contraction of twenty years ago is evident in the 20–30 age group. The pyramid becomes barrel-shaped in the middle age groups, and the tapering above these is very gradual. In contrast with Ceylon or Peru, this pyramid is of a mature society – even the diagram has a middle-age spread. Only 33·3 per cent males and 27·6 per cent females are under 20, but 14·3 per cent and 19·3 per cent respectively are over 60. The population of Israel has an exceptional structure among Asiatic countries because it is so recently derived from Europe. The fact that the majority are immigrants accounts for a lack of balance and for the 'middle-age bulge', but the base is nearer what one would expect in a young agricultural country.

There is another technique of comparing the age-group structures of a large number of countries, and that is by using triangular graph paper. The age characteristics of each country can be summed up by three figures: the percentages of young (under 20), mature (20–59) and old (60 and over). On a triangular graph these three figures can be represented by a single point. The percentage young are plotted along one side, mature along a second and old along the third. When these are projected inwards they meet at one point. Many countries can be plotted on one graph and can in this way be easily compared.

As the graph which is illustrated here shows, in Sweden, for example, the percentage young is 28·75, of mature, 54·75, and of old, 13·50: whereas at the other extreme Colombia has 52·25 per cent young, 42·25 per cent mature and 5·50 per cent old (Fig. 2.4). Other countries range between. This pattern is not haphazard. At one end are the industrial countries of Western Europe, the United States and New Zealand; at the other extreme are the least industrialised, the basically agricultural and peasant countries of Latin America, India, Japan, Turkey and Egypt. Between the extremes are European

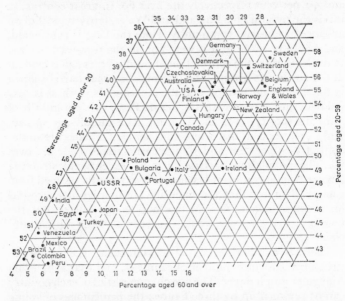

Fig. 2.4. Triangular graph showing percentage young, mature and old in a variety of countries. The emphasis is on older age groups in industrial countries (top, right), and on young age groups in agricultural countries (bottom, left).

countries in which agriculture is still dominant over an increasing industrialisation. Western industrial countries have, in fact, mature populations with many in the older age groups. Agricultural countries are young, with a preponderance of children. In the former a low death rate will ensure that most of the young will eventually fill the older groups: in the latter the higher death rates thin out the ranks very rapidly. In this way the structures vary–and so do the lives of the people; for the different age groups have different demands and different contributions to make, and this alters substantially the total interactions of society and land.

One basic consideration here is the survival–or lack of survival–of children into the age of working for a living, or producing food. This may be shown best by a comparison of survival rates in different age groups in two contrasting societies, India and New Zealand.

| At age | Survival per 100,000 | |
	India	New Zealand
5	60,161	95,212
10	56,467	94,576
15	54,112	94,069
20	51,203	93,217
30	43,931	91,084
40	34,563	88,365
50	24,348	83,328
60	14,933	73,472
70	7,036	54,184
Average working life	30	40

In India, at the age of 15, only 54,112 have survived of each 100,000 children born: in New Zealand 94,069 have survived. The effective labour force is potentially much greater in New Zealand. This illustrates the very high wastage of life in India, and the drain both on family resources and on the community in general. 45,000 children in every 100,000 have to be cared for for periods varying from a few days to 15 years who will contribute nothing to the economy. Put in another way, to produce the same labour force as New Zealand, India must provide twice the number of babies and care for them during their childhood. This is costly in food and resources; yet it is fairly typical of peasant communities, where the family is an economic unit and where sufficient children must be born to ensure constant numbers in the labour force. An echo of this persisted in our own society in Victorian times when a high infant mortality was normal, and parents spoke, not of the children they bore, but of the number they had reared, accepting the waste of life involved in the process of ensuring a large number of survivors.

Advanced industrial societies have, by today, exchanged this problem for another. At one end of the life-span the time spent in formal education is increasing, thus delaying entry into the labour force for an ever-increasing number of people: at the other end of the span early retirement coupled with increased life expectation means an increasing number of non-producing dependants. Compare, for example, the percentages in several age groups in the labour forces of Turkey and the United States:

PERCENTAGE OF AGE GROUPS IN LABOUR FORCE

	10–14	*15–19*	*20–64*	*65 and over*
Turkey	48·7	80·0	92·0	79·0
U.S.A.	1·2	40·0	92·0	42·0

Society in the U.S.A. must be responsible for those in the younger groups and in the oldest who are not economically productive. Even so, the burden cast on the active workers is much less than in a peasant society with its constant demands for replacement. Moreover, the labour force of a peasant society is usually an inefficient one: men and women working in the fields are racked by disease, weakened by hunger and malnutrition, low in energy and often too lethargic to consider ways of leaving the vicious circle of high birth rate and high death rate.

The population of any country, then, is more than just a number of people; it is a distinctive group, a society, with its own structure, its own way of life, its own problems of waste and inefficiency, and its peculiar burdens of the very young and very old. These factors must be appreciated by a geographer, though to sum up these complex conditions and to classify 'quality' is difficult. The U.N.O. has classified countries into groups according to fertility and mortality, ranging from countries with high fertility and high mortality to those with low fertility and low mortality. Professor Stamp has used similar indices to produce fewer and broader categories, and these sum up some of the population characteristics of various countries.

1. The 'old' countries of north-west Europe: low fertility and low mortality: an ageing population but one whose level of living is high enough to support the young and the old non-employed dependants.

2. The countries of Asia and Africa: high fertility and high, or only recently declining, mortality: the population pyramid has a very broad base, wastage is very high and the labour force is not very efficient.

3. Latin America: an increasing population, sharing many of the characteristics of the second group, but where mortality is moderate only against a high fertility.

4. The 'new' countries of the world, North America and Australasia, which are young and growing because the mortality is low but the fertility is higher than in the 'old' countrie. of Europe.

SUGGESTIONS FOR FURTHER READING

J. BEAUJEU-GARNIER: *A Geography of Population* (Methuen), 1966.

C. CLARK: *Population Growth and Land Use* (Macmillan), 1967.

J. I. CLARK: *Population Geography* (Pergamon), 1965.

C. M. CIPOLLA: *Economic History of World Population* (Penguin), 1964.

F. H. OSBORN: *Population* (Population Council), New York, 1958.

E. J. RUSSELL: *World Population and World Food Supplies* (Allen and Unwin), 1956.

L. D. STAMP: *Our Developing World* (Faber and Faber), 1960.

U.N.O.: *Demographic Year Books*.

W. ZELINSKY: *Prologue to Population Geography* (Prentice-Hall), 1966.

Chapter 3

DIVISIONS OF MANKIND

3.1 PHYSICAL BASES OF RACIAL GROUPS

Among the most fundamental differences which distinguish societies from one another are those which are connected with man's physical nature: the basic division of mankind is into races. It will be argued later that the real significance even of race is social, but for the moment it is necessary to begin our classification of mankind along these purely anthropological lines.

What is race? The word is much maligned. It has been so wrongly used in recent history that it is difficult to divest it of distasteful associations. But it must be retrieved so that it can be used in its proper scientific sense. A constant difficulty is the lay habit of using the word loosely and lazily for so many different concepts. People will talk of the human race, meaning mankind as a whole: of the Jewish race when they mean the Jewish people or religion: of Latin races when they mean people with a common group of languages.

A race is a major division of mankind and is defined solely by physical characteristics. It is the final subdivision in the animal world of a series of biological classes beginning with the order Primates. There are three suborders in the Primates, one of which is the Anthropoidea. This suborder is further divided into two divisions; one of these gave rise to the South American monkeys, the other gave rise in Africa and Asia to several families. One of these, Simeidi, included the Gibbon, Orang, Gorilla and Chimpanzee; another, Hominidae, as the name suggests, was human-like. This family had a unique combination of five characteristics which ensured the evolution of man: (i) erect posture; (ii) free-moving arms and hands; (iii) sharp focussing of the eyes; (iv) a superior brain; and (v) powers of speech. Many kinds of man emerged from this family, some of them possibly over-specialised in one way or another and sub-sequently dying out. These are known for their fossil remains, and among them are Java man (*Pithecanthropus erectus*), Peking man (*Sinanthropus pekinensis*), and South African ape-man (*Australopithecus*). Some of these were similar enough to modern man to belong to the same genus, *Homo*; such was Neanderthal man (*Homo neanderthaliensis*), Rhodesian man (*Homo rhodesiensis*), and many others. It is possible that it was the least specialised of all which eventually gave rise to the species *Homo sapiens*, and recent discoveries in Kenya suggest a very long history indeed to this species.

This long lineage emphasises that man is an animal and belongs to a classified system which is common to all animals. *Homo sapiens* is merely one class among many, a subdivision of larger classes, linked to others in an evolutionary sequence. Race, scientifically speaking, is nothing more than one further subdivision, and the classification of races must rest solely on the same scientific basis as the remainder of the biological system. The criteria on which the classification of race is based must be (i) visible features; (ii) measurable; and (iii) inherited from a common ancestor: furthermore the anthropologist looks for the characteristics of a group, averaging the innumerable variations of individual people. An American anthropologist has defined race in this way: 'A race is a great subdivision of mankind, members of which, though varying individually, are characterised as a group by a certain combination of measurable features which have been derived from a common ancestor.'

What are the features which the anthropologist measures in order to make his classification? The important ones include skin colour, stature, shape of head, face, nose, eye and type of hair.

(1) Skin colour. We speak glibly of white, black and yellow races, and this is indeed a primary division of mankind. But it is also an over-simplification. Skin colour depends on a number of variables, such as the amount of pigment (melanin) in the skin, the depth of the blood capillaries under the skin, and the thickness of the epidermis and the cuticle. Some pigment is

almost always present (exceptional individuals who lack any pigment are called *albino*); but if the quantity is very small and the blood vessels can be seen underneath, then a pinkish white colour results. Sunbathing may intensify the melanin and bring it nearer the surface, giving a tanned appearance to so-called white people, but this is temporary. Little melanin and deep-seated blood vessels allows the parchment colour of the epidermis itself to be dominant, as among the so-called yellow races. Heavy pigmentation gives dark shades of brown.

(2) Stature is easily measured and classified into short, medium and tall. With exceptions the male range is between about 130 cm/4 ft 3 in. and 200 cm/6 ft 7 in, the female range from 120 cm/4 ft 0 in to 187 cm/6 ft 2 in. Within limits food or the lack of food can effect stature, but it is nevertheless an inherited quality.

(3) The shape of the head, expressed as an index of breadth over length × 100 (the *cephalic index*), is a standard criterion. Under 78·5 is considered a long head (*dolichocephalic*), 78·6 to 82·5 is medium (*mesocephalic*), more than 82·5 is broad (*brachycephalic*).

(4) The shape of face gives a variety of features. It can be long or broad, the chin jutting out (*prognathous*) or receding (*orthognathous*).

(5) The shape of the nose. An index of the ratio of nose width at the nostrils to its length × 100 enables us to differentiate between long narrow noses (less than 70), medium noses (70–84) and short flat noses (over 84). Coupled with the long nose is the existence of a distinct bridge, whereas the broad nose is often depressed. Variations in shape are very considerable.

(6) The eye. Eye colour can be classified in the same way as skin colour. But even more significant is the shape of the eye, for in this respect Mongoloids differ from other races. The upper fold of the Mongoloid eye droops over to give the impression of a slit-like opening. This is the *epicanthic fold*, and when it is more emphasised at the inner corner of the eye it tends to give the impression of an outward and upward slant,

often accentuated because of the comparative absence of browridges and eyebrows in Mongoloids.

(7) Hair. Although there is a multitude of hair forms, they can be conveniently grouped into three classes: (a) straight hair, long and lank and rigid, and round in cross section; (b) wavy hair, and (c) kinky or woolly hair, much flatter in cross section, and emerging from its follicle in a spiral, and in extreme cases forming hard tufts. Colour, again depending on the amount of melanin in the hair, sometimes mixed with a red pigment, varies from ash blond (no melanin) and strawberry blond (much red pigment), to black (great amount of melanin).

These are some of the main features which are measured by the anthropologist. Even on these characteristics the number of possible variations must seem, at first glance, to be infinite. If one feature alone were used, then we would have very few races; for instance skin colour would give three groups: Caucasoid (white), Mongoloid (yellow) and Negroid (black). But within any one of these, say Negroid, stature can vary from short to tall, and within either of these, head form can vary. Theoretically the number of combinations is immense. But in fact the number is cut down by the linkage of many of these characteristics, a linkage which suggests a common origin, and which is the only justification for attempting a classification at all. Woolly hair and black hair-colour go together, as do black skin and a broad nose: fair hair is usually wavy and goes with fair skin: and so on. It is the combination of measurable features which enables us to sort out a seeming mass of heterogeneous human beings into the divisions we call races: and these are always generalised for a group. Individual peculiarities must be forgotten – as indeed they are when we are viewing racial groups other than our own. To the European all Chinese look alike, because only the marked differences between European and Chinese are noticed.

The table which appears on the following page gives the main characteristics of the three great racial groups.

The three groups are known as *primary* races, but there are people who show mixtures of these basic characteristics which suggest that at some time after the establishment

Main Characteristics of the World's Major Races

Trait	Caucasoid	Mongoloid	Negroid
Skin colour	Pale reddish white to olive-brown	Saffron to yellow-brown; some reddish brown	Brown to brown-black; some yellow-brown
Stature	Medium to tall	Medium short to medium tall	Very short to tall
Head form	Long to broad and short; medium high to very high	Predominantly broad; medium high	Predominantly long; low to medium high
Face	Narrow to medium broad; no prognathism	Medium broad to very broad	Medium broad to narrow; strong prognathism
Nose	Usually high bridge; narrow to medium broad	Low to medium bridge; medium broad	Low to medium bridge; broad to very broad
Eyes	Light blue to dark brown; occasional lateral eye-fold	Brown to dark brown; medial epicanthic fold common	Brown to brown-black; vertical eye-fold common
Hair	Head: light blond to dark brown, fine to medium texture and straight to wavy Body: moderate to profuse	Head: brown to black, coarse texture and straight Body: sparse	Head: brown-black to black, coarse texture and curly to woolly/frizzy
Body build	Linear to lateral; slender to rugged	Tends to lateral; some linearity	Tends to lateral and muscular; some linearity

of the fundamental differences groups mixed and produced permanent strains with characteristics from two of the primary races. These are sometimes known as *composite races*. The Australian aborigines have a predominantly white base, of archaic type, mixed with Negroid: central Pacific peoples are mainly Mongoloid with mixture of Caucasoid, but the Papuan-Melanesian peoples are basically Negroid. The Bushmen Hottentot are basically Negroid too, but mixed with very early *Homo* strains.

Having disposed of this very broad outline of racial classes a geographer turns naturally to their distribution. Fig. 3.1 shows the position before the great age of discovery: it shows what

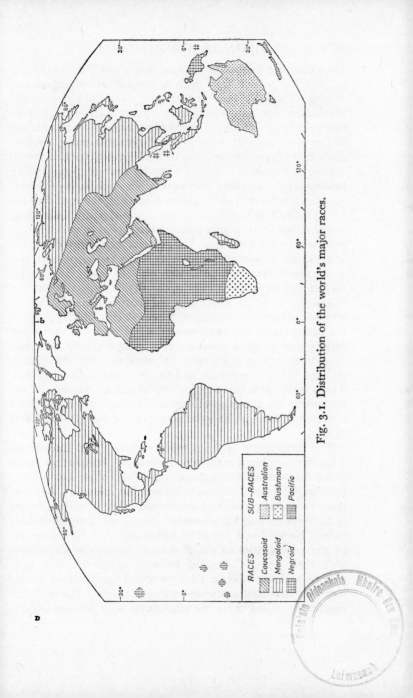

Fig. 3.1. Distribution of the world's major races.

RACES
Caucasoid
Mongoloid
Negroid

SUB-RACES
Australian
Bushman
Pacific

D

are called the indigenous populations, though obviously this distribution is itself the result of prehistoric movement and mixing. The later historic spread of Caucasoid people, the peopling of the New World from Europe since the 17th century, would give much too confused a picture. The distribution of the three primary races is straightforward enough. Africa south of the Sahara is the home of the Negroids: the Caucasoids extend in a wide belt from north-west Europe to the Indian subcontinent, including northern Africa and parts of Asiatic Russia. Siberia, east and south-east Asia and the Americas are Mongoloid. This distribution, together with our knowledge of racial movements, suggests that *Homo sapiens* spread from an area within the Caucasoid belt, possibly somewhere vaguely in southern Russia: that in moving south and north-east, this early undifferentiated man was able to make two major adaptations to the environment, one to the hot wet climates of inter-tropical Africa where Negroid characteristics developed, and one to the cold climates of the north-east which produced the Mongoloids. The latter crossed a landbridge at the Bering Straits and peopled America at a comparatively late date (15,000 to 20,000 years ago), i.e. after the physical characteristics of the Mongoloids had become genetically stabilised. There were, then, three major Old World adaptations to environment by a comparatively undifferentiated early *Homo sapiens*, together with an extension of one of these into the New World.

The distribution of the composite races is also interesting. They are peripheral to the supposed centre of dispersion. Some claim that a marginal location, sometimes coupled with isolation, would in itself promote changes: but it is also a fact that these marginal races show admixture, often of earlier strains of *Homo* which may have been less specialised. Some such mixture of Negroid and pre-*Homo sapiens* characteristics gave rise to the peculiarities of the Bushmen. Australian aborigines, with their paler Caucasoid features, make the link with Europe and the Middle East via the Dravidians of India. Negroids extended eastward to Papua, but by the time the Pacific is reached there are admixtures with Mongoloid and even with sub-branches of the Caucasoid races. Perhaps the most spectacular of the isolated groups is the Ainu of north Japan, a branch of the Caucasoid race; their location shows the possibilities of movement as well as the way in which racial features may be preserved far from the point of origin. The mixing of racial characteristics, the result of the free movement of man before as well as after the physical adaptations of his body to the earth's varied climate, is often preserved by the isolation of many of these peripheral areas.

The picture looks a comparatively simple one. Of course it over-simplifies the facts. Each primary race has its sub-divisions. The Negroids, for example, are divided into the Negro, the very tall Nilotic and the short Negrito. There are four main sub-races of the Caucasoids in Europe: Nordic, Mediterranean, Alpine and East Baltic. Individuals belonging to the first are typically tall, slender, big-boned, with a fairly long and lofty head, a narrow face, prominent chin and narrow nose and lips. They are blue-eyed blonds, whose hair is fine and straight to wavy in type. They are found mainly in north European peoples, in Scandinavia (where remnants of the classical type are found), lowland Britain, northern France, the Low Countries, northern Germany and Finland. Mediter-ranean peoples are shorter, long-headed, dark in colouring with dark eyes and black hair. Their name suggests their main distribution, but they also extend through Brittany to form a major element in western Britain. Indeed they form a basic racial substratum in the British Isles, but they were displaced and overlain by Nordic invaders in the east and south in historic times. Alpines are broad-headed, have broad squarish faces, concave noses and abundant dark wavy hair. They are medium in stature and stocky in build. They are found in a belt from France to the U.S.S.R., where they form a dominant element in the Slav population. The East Baltic group shows a mixture of Alpine and Nordic characteristics.

3.2 SOCIAL BASES OF RACIAL GROUPS

It is essential to remember the limitations of maps of racial distribution. Two are especially important.

1. The world map suggests permanent zones. A moment's reflection on man's great mobility reminds one of how blurred these divisions are on the earth's surface. The distribution shown in the map is that of the late 15th century. Today Nordics, and to a lesser extent the other Caucasoid sub-races, have submerged the aboriginal peoples in practically the whole of North America, large tracts of South America, South Africa and Australasia. Within Europe, progressively increasing mobility has erased any racial boundaries that might once have existed. It is true to say that in any population one can only abstract racial characteristics from a large group of very heterogeneous individuals. Rarely are there whole populations in the Western world which retain common racial characteristics. Our definition of racial groups is based on average measurements.

2. This is because mobility has led to crossbreeding and this in its turn has made nonsense of any idea of a pure race. With every preceding generation the forebears of any individual multiply in a geometric progression. If a person today can trace his family back for eight generations, it means that his genetic constitution, and consequently his physical build, is derived from 512 ancestors who lived about 1700: admixture is so probable, even in so short a span, that racial purity becomes a meaningless term.

It is small wonder that the layman is confused about the concept of race. The anthropological ideas we have discussed above are scientific but limited: the categories are to a large extent abstract and very difficult to apply to small groups of people. The anthropologist describes groups not individuals. Yet the layman has broadened the term race until it has become almost meaningless. He has, in addition, often ascribed to his own race a 'superiority'–implicitly a mental superiority–for which there is no evidence. These misconceptions have led to tragic chapters in man's history: small wonder that the very word 'race' has undesirable overtones.

But if the scientific concept of race tends to be an abstract, and if the distribution maps are so generalised, have racial characteristics no significance? Is the anthropological classification merely an academic exercise? Not entirely. The generalisations must be made: the group characteristics do exist: and they are relevant because the lay misconceptions are hung on these very hooks. Strange as it may seem, we must now turn to these lay misconceptions for it is on these that human interactions are based.

However diffident an anthropologist might be, even after extensive observations, to classify a person who has mixed racial characteristics, a layman will often make an unhesitating judgement. To some extent he must, because his behaviour in any given circumstance will depend upon such a snap judgement: it does not follow that his judgement will agree with the anthropologist's, but his is the one which will count in the circumstance. His classes are rigid. He thinks in terms of black and white. How does he deal with the inbetween cases, the racial mixtures? In the way in which he has been taught. If he comes from the southern states of the United States he will see any person with *any* observable Negroid features as black: indeed he may go further and fall back on known Negroid characteristics in the person's forebears to call an apparently white person black. Almost the reverse of this is true in South America, where a *few* observable Caucasoid features are enough for acceptance into the white group. From a layman's point of view race is what people have been taught it is: it is culturally defined. One American anthropologist puts it this way: 'A race is a group of people with more or less permanent distinguishing characteristics to which persons concerned attach certain interpretations.'

Certain physical features are used for rapid identification, and this is necessary to permit group cohesion. Man consciously groups himself, or classifies himself, but never objectively. His fundamental division of mankind is into two groups—'those who are like me, and those who are not'. 'Those who are not' are in the first place those who *look* different, so he attaches his label to a racial feature. The most obvious is colour, but stature, hair form and facial characteristics are all important. This is very far from the anthropologist's average measurements, but we are now dealing with the *real* bases of divisions, however far they may be from scientific truths, however dependent on error, misunderstanding and myth. For these half truths have been learned from previous generations and go back beyond the logical world of the scientist. Moreover, they are judgements and classifications which are often not physical and not inherited. An anthropologist has no evidence of differences in intelligence among racial groups; yet this is a supposed difference which appeals greatly to most peoples. 'We' are always mentally superior. Such values are cultural. In fact differences in intelligence are always very great between members of a single group, but difficult to assess between several groups. Intelligent, unintelligent, superior, inferior; all these are concepts about individuals, but they are spuriously attached to groups. Ethnocentricity, i.e. awareness of one's own ethnic (racial–cultural) group, emphasises the differences between groups, and often expresses it as antipathy to all other groups.

There is some excuse for this misleading, and often painful, characterisation of all groups other than one's own. It was suggested above that the layman's snap decision is based on some immediately apparent feature: he must be taught to do this, because he wishes his behaviour in a given situation to accord with that which has been taught to him, and because his chances of approaching the problem logically are infinitely remote. He has a shorthand method of classifying, not only racial appearance, but all the cultural elements of other ethnic groups. He has been taught that certain people dress in a certain way, talk peculiarly, have certain mannerisms. He has a ready-made picture of an individual from any other society. These 'stereotypes' are, of course, by their very nature caricatures, but they do mean (*a*) that communication is made easier and (*b*) that groups are easily if roughly classified. All English people carry a mental picture of a 'typical' Frenchman, a 'typical' Jew, a 'typical' American. However grossly misleading the images, passed on in a hundred and one unconscious ways to succeeding generations, they are the means of making a snap judgement: and they also save a lot of verbal description if one refers in passing to, for example, a 'Frenchman'.

3.3 CULTURAL DIFFERENCES

The cultural elements–i.e. those ideas which have been passed on from one generation to the other–figure so largely in the kind of classification discussed above that we are justified in basing fundamental subdivisions of mankind on these. It is more real to talk of ethnic groups than of racial groups, and although racial characteristics play a large part in determining ethnic groups, the latter are also based on cultural characteristics. Divisions in mankind can be most rigid when based on ways of living and thinking, and such divisions usually count for more than the broad racial classes.

One of the most important elements that binds people together is language. Difference in language is an immediate bar to communication between groups. Someone who 'speaks another language', even in the colloquial sense, is not one of 'us'. Language is the medium through which ideas are transmitted, so that one can expect a certain amount of homogeneity in the culture of common language groups. The world distribution of languages is very complex, for although many of them come from common stocks, the similarities which linguistic scholars emphasise are lost on the individual groups who tend, if anything, to stress very minor differences. Differences even of dialect are enough to divide people. 'Speaking another language' can often signify even small nuances of meaning.

There are in Europe alone over thirty major languages, each the basis of an ethnic or cultural group. One need go no farther than the British Isles to see a considerable diversity in languages which was formerly even more marked (Fig. 3.2). Nearly one person in three in Wales still speaks Welsh, and the language is the core of the separate identity of this group, the basis of a literature and the medium of certain ideas, traditions, etc., which are not shared with other groups. The remnants of Gaelic in Scotland are enough to remind us of one of the bases of separateness in the north, and few would deny that loss of language has completely obliterated these differences. Irish is still spoken in the western counties of Ireland and is the

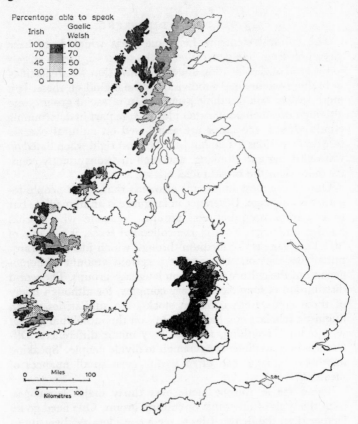

Percentage able to speak

Irish	Gaelic Welsh
100	100
70	70
45	50
30	30
0	0

Fig. 3.2. Distribution of Celtic languages in the British Isles.

official state language. Manx has almost died out and Cornish is now fossilised in text-books. To some extent these Celtic languages can be grouped. There are basic similarities between Gaelic, Irish and Manx, the so-called q-Celts; and between Welsh and Cornish and Breton–the p-Celts. The people concerned are nevertheless distinct groups, and whether the language be alive, on the wane, or nearly extinct, one still recognises Welshmen, Scotsmen, Irishmen and Manxmen. Indeed, these groups have, or have had, separate political lives and their conquest by England was relatively late in their history. Ireland has re-emerged as a completely separate state: the Northern Irish, a mixture of Irish, Scots and English, have their own parliament, and so has the Isle of Man.

Religious beliefs are very deep-seated, sometimes uniting peoples of different racial and language groups, often dividing peoples who are otherwise identical. The earliest beliefs were animistic – i.e. they consisted of nature worship of one kind or another – and there are still many residual areas of this type of religion among the simpler peoples of the world. The origins of more advanced beliefs are linked with the great civilisations of the Old World and today have certain distribution patterns (Fig. 3.3) which suggest their diffusion.

Hinduism, very closely linked with India, is a comprehensive religious system which embraces belief in many gods at one extreme and belief in one absolute being at the other; but the whole is welded together by certain fundamental attitudes such as worship of cattle, a doctrine of rebirth, and the caste system. The last makes rigid certain occupational differences, and was probably introduced to identify, first, groups of conquerors from the conquered, and later all the grades of division of labour. There is, then, a practical social element in Hinduism – one which further divides the society – as well as a system of belief and philosophy. The latter seemed so remote to Siddhattha Gautama (the Buddha), who lived in the 6th century B.C., that he founded a new religion which now embraces many millions in south-east Asia. His answer to the world's problems was a retreat into non-existence, and this may well seem attractive in a part of the world where existence is often at a miserably low level. China has two other religions, Confucianism and Taoism. The teachings of Confucius (551–478 B.C.) are concerned with social relationships, welded onto a more primitive system of beliefs which include ancestor worship. Lao Tze, a contemporary of Confucius, fastened on the spiritual and mystic elements in this primitive sub-stratum to teach a passive religion (Taoism). Japan has its own system

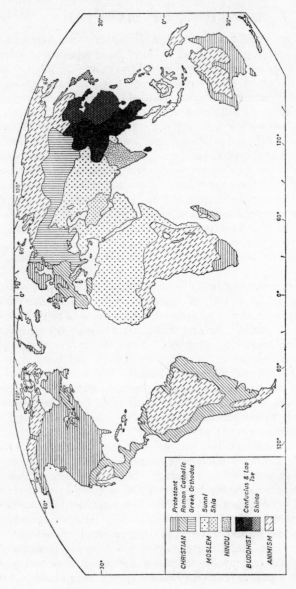

Fig. 3.3. Distribution of the world's major religions.

CHRISTIAN
Protestant
Roman Catholic
Greek Orthodox

MOSLEM
Sunni
Shia

HINDU

BUDDHIST
Confucius & Lao Tse
Shinto

ANIMISM

of beliefs, Shinto, basically a primitive animistic religion, given a deeper significance by the infusion of Buddhism in the 6th century A.D.

The other three great world religions, Judaism, Christianity and Islam, all arose in the Middle East, Christianity emerging from Judaism in what is now Israel, and Islam emerging in Arabia and owing something to both other religions. Judaism survived the break-up of the Jewish nation into minority sects in the cities of the Western world and the Middle East. Since the formation of the state of Israel it has re-emerged as a state religion almost at its point of origin. Both Christianity and Islam have spread remarkably. Christianity became a basic element in Western culture and spread into the New World with European overseas expansion, until its adherents now dominate four continents. The early spread of Islam was even more spectacular. Within a short time of the death of Mohammed (A.D. 632) his teachings had spread to the Indus and over the whole of North Africa, a main element in Arab civilisation. It spread temporarily into Spain, but in Europe today there are only a few remnant groups in the Balkans.

In more detail the divisions of Christianity and Islam reveal interesting distribution patterns. There is a sharp cleavage in Islam between Sunni and Shia, and the fact that the latter are dominant in Iran and in part of eastern Iraq has had important political consequences as a barrier to Arab unity. The division of Christianity into Roman Catholicism and Protestantism is equally marked. In Europe the former predominates in the Mediterranean countries, France and Ireland, and the latter predominates in Northern Europe. The Christian church has a third strong element derived from the eastern Mediterranean, that is the Greek Orthodox church which is predominant in south-east Europe and in Russia. Predominantly Roman Catholic South America and Protestant North America reflect stages in the conquest of those countries and the cultures of the peoples who settled them. Canada retains its very strong enclave of Roman Catholicism in Quebec, reflecting the religion of its 17th-century French settlers; and vast numbers of south and east European migrants have greatly increased the proportion of Roman Catholics in north-eastern U.S.A.

It was stressed above that within the British Isles the Irish, Scots, Welsh and Manx have retained their identity because they originally had different languages and different cultures. But they are also groups which are identified with certain *areas* of the British Isles: Ireland, Scotland, Wales, Man. This is not necessarily true of all ethnic groups. At an earlier stage in man's history, when movement and instability were the rule rather than the exception, it was true of no ethnic group. The primary thing which distinguished such a group was social cohesion. This originated in ties of kinship: a person belonged to a certain group, irrespective of where they lived. A Jew was a Jew in any European country for those long centuries when he had no home of his own. But at some stage, probably in medieval times in Europe, a subtle change became apparent. As the historian Maine put it—'England was once the country in which Englishmen lived: Englishmen are now the people who inhabit England.' There has been a transference of emphasis from social group to territory: whereas once a person was born into a specific society, now he is born within specific political boundaries.

This has far-reaching consequences. It brings us to a very recent stage, possibly the most advanced, in man's organisation. We began this chapter with a biological classification, then discussed social groups based on cultural differences; we must now deal with groups based on one element only in those cultural differences—the political. The classifications are not mutually exclusive: racial elements often underlie ethnic groups and ethnic differences underlie political differences: but there are also examples of several ethnic groups lying within one political division. But the last political grouping, with all the sanction of law and ideas of sovereignty, may well be the strongest of all.

3.4 ETHNIC GROUPS

The subdivisions of mankind based on political organisation are the ones with which we are most familiar and are probably the most advanced and complex of all. They have by no means obliterated the other divisions, racial and ethnic, which have been dealt with, but what has often happened is that many ethnic problems have become subsidiary to state problems. Even problems of racial differences may well be contained within one state, although they may also often become world issues. The United States, although politically one unit, is deeply involved with all major racial groups, a fact which is emphasised in its own census with its primary division of the population into White, Black, Yellow and Red (even this classification, let alone its application, does not necessarily accord with anthropological classification): South Africa is similarly concerned with two major races. Australia is no less concerned to maintain a so-called 'racially pure' population. The United States is also concerned with numerous ethnic groups, for in the last 150 years every country in Europe has contributed to its very heterogeneous population. Very many countries have ethnic problems, not only because of the movement of people but because the drawing of new boundaries so often creates so-called 'minority groups'. Both racial groups and ethnic groups of this kind, which have no territory of their own but are merely parts of a larger, different population, are of great interest to anthropologists, sociologists and social geographers. The political geographer too must be aware of these problems and their consequences: not only because the location of such groups and their spatial relations are interesting but because of the part they play in the life of the state.

The attitude of a state towards other peoples and the degree to which it controls their movement affects the distribution of racial and ethnic groups. The White Australian Policy, aimed at the strictest control of people entering Australia in an effort to keep the population white, or even British, has a profound effect on the distribution of population in Oceania and southeast Asia. For if this movement were unchecked there would undoubtedly be Asiatic migration and an extension of southeast Asian economy into Australia. The Australians look upon this as their main 'racial' problem for they can almost ignore the small number, about 50,000, of surviving aboriginals.

The United States faces the problems of ethnic as well as racial minority groups. Its own aboriginal peoples are now confined to reserves, their economies fossilised in the pages of text-books, they themselves museum specimens exploited by tourists and anthropologists. Their segregation is a measure of group antipathy based on radical differences in cultural level. The United States also has a small number of Asiatics, particularly on the west coast, but their immigration was drastically regulated at the end of the last century. The negro population is the greatest 'alien' element, and the attitude of the white majority to this group is that of a rigid caste, based on social definitions attached to racial characteristics. The negro population is derived from a slave population, a cultural difference difficult to eradicate. A population of 750,000 in 1790 had given rise to 19 million by 1960. Until the latter part of the 19th century negroes spread with the extension of the cotton belt. Since emancipation there has been considerable movement to the north, particularly to the northern cities. But whereas a small number of negroes might lose themselves in a large city and provoke very little reaction, the building up of very large groups has resulted in the same restriction of distribution—i.e. segregation—in northern cities as they suffered in the south. In both New York and Chicago in particular, considerable number of negroes are crowded within narrow 'black' belts, giving a very distinctive distribution pattern.

The effort to maintain 'racial purity' is very different from the American attitude towards ethnic groups. These they try to assimilate: indeed, the United States is popularly looked upon as a 'melting pot'. In 1960 there were over 19 million people in the United States who had been born in another country, and 23,800,000 whose parents had been born outside the United States. At the end of the 18th century the vast majority of white Americans could trace their ancestry to the British Isles. The stream of English, Welsh, Scots and Irish continued throughout the last century, augmented by millions of Germans, Scandinavians, French. Towards the end of the century this north-west European flood diminished: it was Italians, Poles and south-east European peoples who came in millions between 1890 and 1914. The 1914–18 war more or less put an end to immigration on this scale. These movements –which are dealt with in greater detail in another chapter– imply the break-away of millions of people from their parent ethnic group, and although some of them regroup in the United States and maintain their own language, religion, traditions, etc., the vast majority lose themselves in a larger social milieu: they are prepared to break their home ties in exchange for the economic advantages of life in the United States. Some return home, of course, but the great majority make the transition, and even if first-generation immigrants– those who were born in another country–find the adaptation difficult, their children rarely fail to become fully-fledged Americans. The relative uniformity of the outward signs of being an American, together with the very rapid rate of change, makes adaptation fairly easy, and the Americans themselves, partly by their educational system, speed this process of Americanisation. The ethnic groups need not lose their identity completely and often add an indefinable quality and an enrichment to American life. The older groups have been absorbed the most and their distribution tends to be the same as the distribution of the population in general–with the exception of their absence in the southern states. But there are still interesting concentrations of Scandinavians in Wisconsin, for example, and a few north-east industrial towns have much more than their share of Welsh or German people. The newer immigrants are more confined to the north-east in general and to the cities in particular.

In time all these ethnic groups are bound to lose their identity almost entirely, for they have no internal cohesion strong enough to counter the attractions and advancements of American life.

This solution of absorption does not apply to the same degree north of the 49th parallel, where, within one federated state, there are two major ethnic groups–Canadians and French Canadians. The latter, derived almost entirely from an original French population of 60,000 which had settled in Quebec by the mid-17th century, are adamant on maintaining their cultural separateness. Often markedly anti-British and anti-American, and having had no ties with post-revolution France, they sometimes express this by suggesting 'Latin' links, mainly religious and cultural, with Latin American states. In Quebec the imprint of a former French tenure system is clearly seen in the landscape, in the long strip farms, in the street villages. French is still spoken and Roman Catholicism is the religion of the vast majority. Ottawa, federal capital, sits on the boundary of British Canada and French Canada, and, politically at least, subtly unites them.

3.5 POLITICAL GROUPS—THE STATE

The political map of the world is one of the most familiar to students of geography. On the face of it the formation of states is a very acceptable division of the earth's surface and a convenient classification of its people, in spite of the fact that it is constantly changing. But further consideration shows the many problems which are involved in this political subdivision. To begin with, although a state boundary line is so very easy to delimit on the map, it is much more difficult to demarcate on the ground: indeed most of those precisely drawn lines on the political map of the world have never been demarcated. It is even misleading to think of the divisions as being lines. The 'line' is much more often a zone, or a frontier. At first glance an island may seem to be an ideal unit for one state. But even a coast-line is really a zone. Not only is there a small intertidal zone, not only is there sometimes the no-man's-land of quarantine, or an Ellis Island, but territorial sovereignty extends beyond the land, and over the sea; formerly to fairly well-accepted limits of three nautical miles, but now over very varying and indeterminate distances. In the past states have dominated far beyond even this. The Mediterranean was *Mare Nostrum* to the Romans, Venice collected dues from all who used the Adriatic, and Tudor England claimed sovereignty of the Narrow Seas from Norway to Spain.

To return to land-locked states, the geographer is interested to see to what extent physical features are related to frontiers and boundaries (Fig. 3.4). If mountains are high enough they

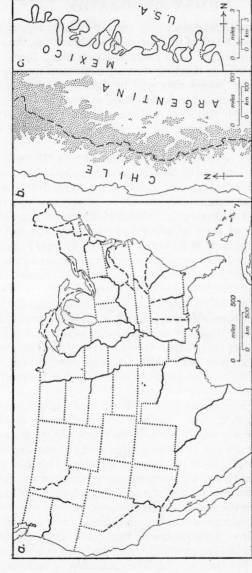

Fig. 3.4. Types of boundaries. The vast majority of state boundaries in the U.S.A. (a) are along either rivers or lines of reference. That between Chile and Argentine (b) is a good example of a mountain boundary. The Rio Grande (c) shows the disadvantages of a river boundary, the dotted line showing agreed compromises which ignore the shifting meanders.

E

make good frontiers because they are unpopulated regions and less likely to be bones of contention. The Himalayas, the Alps and the Pyrenees, all have major frontiers along them. Yet there are pitfalls in thinking that all mountains make good frontiers. Lower ranges may well be the homes of mountain communities: even in the Andes, large communities of people live at very high altitudes. And even in the high ranges the boundary becomes important at passes, which are low and vital to trade.

When new countries were first opened up to European expansion, rivers seemed to be very acceptable boundaries: they were easily recognised, and involved no demarcation. Such boundaries are commonly found in many newly settled countries. But their relative absence in Europe is significant, for hundreds of years of adjustment, by wars and treaties, have shown the river to be a poor boundary for many reasons. In a developed country a river is usually the centre of a social unit, a valley, and to split such a unit is unwise. In the United States, where the Mississippi and Missouri separate several states there are often towns on either bank, e.g. the two St. Louis, two Kansas Cities, Council Bluffs and Omaha. It is only the federal union of all these states which makes these river boundaries acceptable. An international boundary on a river can be critical, particularly when its water is used, e.g. some of the Punjab rivers: and the use of the river by transport is easier if controlled by one state.

Physically a river can play tricks on men's efforts at state demarcation. A mature river like the Rio Grande, dividing the United States and Mexico, is constantly changing course. Oxbow lakes are cut off leaving large tracts of territory–and communities of people–in another country. This has happened so often that these two countries have agreed on certain legal readjustments so that the state boundary is no longer entirely along the line of the river.

One of the most common boundary lines in new countries is the straight line. Such geometric boundaries are particularly useful in so-called 'empty lands', and are often retained after the country has been settled. They are lines of latitude and longitude, and are particularly prominent in North America and Australia. The most famous is the 49th parallel, the dominating east–west boundary between the United States and Canada. This is the easiest kind of line to delimit, though not always so easy to demarcate. A similar line running across a very densely populated country, as in Korea, leads to considerable confusion and hardship.

These are the most common types of boundaries. Their classification and evolution are of interest to the political geographer: their delimitation is vital to society. For in those parts of the earth which are densely populated, like Europe, and where constant movement has blurred ethnic distinctions, it is very difficult indeed to define boundaries which do not conflict with the interest of some groups or other. Minorities are often created by boundary delimitation, i.e. pockets of one ethnic or language group are caught within the national boundaries of another, usually because strategic and economic considerations are uppermost in boundary-making. Tension is inevitable. The shift in allegiance of Alsace and Lorraine to Germany in 1871, and back to France after the First World War, had a great effect on the society, made worse by the fact that the population was already a mixed one. An Austrian minority in the Italian Tyrol, the result of a transfer of territory after the First World War, has created tension since. Such problems are legion in Eastern Europe where boundaries have been reshaped several times in this century. Indeed this region of instability is often called the 'shatter zone', for boundary changes, minority problems, and economic and political instability often go together.

The ideal would be to have a homogeneous population within each state boundary: in reality most boundaries are strategically determined and ignore all social facts. The political map of India has undergone remarkable changes since 1947, moving towards an ideal, even if imperfectly (Fig. 3.5). Under British domination India was a vast collection of states, some small, some very large. Britain exercised direct control over many of these, which together made up British India: with the remainder she had treaties defining her relationship

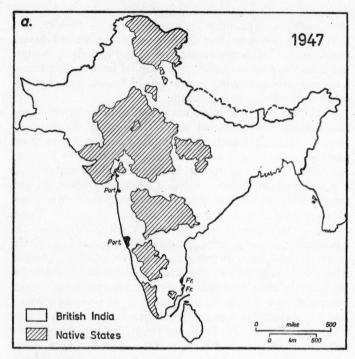

a.

1947

British India

Native States

Port.

Port.

Fr.
Fr.

0   miles   500
0   km   500

Fig. 3.5.

with the native princes who kept a certain degree of sovereignty. In this division into British India and the princely states, the former was determined strategically, i.e. with few exceptions Britain directly controlled the coast, the two great river valleys, and the north-west frontier; and ensured that this directly controlled territory split up the major native states in such a way that they had no contact one with the other. In 1947 India was partitioned in a very different way. The basis was religious, for the new state of Pakistan was based on Moslem majorities. This, incidentally, gave rise to a Western and an Eastern Pakistan, separated from each other by India. This partition was a realistic appraisal of a vital difference in

Fig. 3.5. (a) In pre-partition India the major native states were isolated and dominated by British India. This strategic pattern has been replaced by one based on religion and language (b).

two cultures, expressed as religion. In 1958 India took the next logical step and rearranged her own internal state boundaries on the basis of language. This was difficult, and, as with the religious solution, it involved creating some minorities, many of them discontented. But the modern political pattern in India is now a logical one based on cultural variations: imperfect though it is it reflects Indian society and culture. It is very different from the imposed British pattern which made no concession to these differences.

Within its international boundary every state exercises

paramount authority by law. This is the sovereignty of states which theoretically makes them all equal. But a geographer is not greatly concerned with this equality. To him it is variety of states–in size, population, economic wealth–which is the most interesting feature of the political map. He is also interested in their origins, growth and expansion.

Most states have within them a nucleus, a centre of manpower and wealth; this is often the area from which, in former times, control has spread to the present boundaries of the state. In Britain, Lowland England, and in particular the London Basin, was such a nucleus. The Paris Basin, similarly, has become dominant in France. Associated with the rise of the nation state was the rise of the capital city, for the wealth of the nuclear region was associated with the growth of the capital city which was almost always its centre. Just as the strength of the state lay in the nucleus, so its wealth and influence became concentrated in the capital. The 16th and 17th centuries saw the beginning of this disproportionate growth of the capital city which is still apparent.

In a way every capital city is unique, but many have points in common which have led to attempts at classification. It is certainly useful to note that besides those, like London and Paris, which lie within the rich lands which gave birth to them, there are capitals which lie outside such nuclear areas. A capital until recently, Istanbul, or Constantinople, had no rich hinterland: in its heyday even its food came from Egypt and the Black Sea. Copenhagen is peripheral in Denmark. In both cases the city's growth was related to former extensions of its territories. Constantinople was the centre of Byzantium: it was a supra-national city: it declined with the decline of the Ottoman Empire, and when Turkey emerged after the First World War as a new state its capital was shifted to Ankara. Similarly, Copenhagen was once the centre of a state that dominated the Baltic Sea.

Other capital cities mark points of contact between societies, or sites where invaders have entered new lands. This is particularly so in the New World where urban civilisation was almost always brought by Europeans. The state capitals of

Australia–Darwin, Brisbane, Sydney, Melbourne, Adelaide, Perth, Hobart–are all on or near the coast, the toeholds of Europeans in a strange land. Bombay, Madras and Calcutta show the dependence of the alien British on naval strength. The early capitals of North America were coastal, though they shifted inland when settlement went beyond the Alleghenies. In South America there is an interesting contrast between the Andean capitals, many above 2,750 m/9,000 ft, which lie in rich basins and were first founded by pre-Columban cultures like the Inca, and the later European toeholds which developed into Buenos Aires, Montevideo and Rio de Janeiro.

Lastly some capitals can be classified as artificial in the sense that they were built purely from political considerations, have little economic base, and have therefore no direct relationship with a state nucleus. Madrid was probably the first of such capitals, its central position a conscious attempt at pulling together the disparate richer regions of Spain which were peripheral. And so, in the 15th century, a lonely outpost on an unattractive and barren plateau gradually began to be transformed into a capital city. The outstanding example of the 18th century is Washington. Washington lay roughly mid-way between northern and southern elements when the newly formed United States was still an Atlantic community. Today it is a good example of the single-purpose city, for half its employed workers are engaged in government, the other half in services. The same desire to balance various political attractions led to the choice of a lonely bush station as the site of Canberra at the beginning of this century. This again is a city which has only one purpose, and whose only justification is federal government. The most recent and exciting artificial capital is Brasilia. Placed well outside the settled areas of Brazil, it is hoped that it will not only be a symbol of Brazil's maturity–the cutting of the link with the coast and thus with the European heritage–but that its central position will be a focus for the several states of Brazil and a growing point for future development.

3.6 GROUPING OF STATES

Washington, Canberra and Brasilia are all federal capitals, a reminder that many states are grouped together into larger entities. The merging of states on an equal footing is a federation. The extension of the authority of an expanding state over other countries, by war or by diplomacy, leads to empires, the different parts of which will have varying degrees of sovereignty. From the disintegration of former empires, new states are continually being formed. Political geography is a dynamic subject, and grouping, disruption and regrouping are constantly taking place. Three of the most extensive and powerful groupings are the British Empire, the United States of America and the Union of Soviet Socialist Republics. Geographically there is much in common between the two latter, and they contrast markedly with the first. Both the U.S.A. and the U.S.S.R. are continental, i.e. their hegemony extends almost entirely over a single land mass. The United States expanded by acquisition of territory in the first half of the 19th century from its Atlantic seaboard origins to the Pacific. The U.S.S.R. expanded from its European core into Siberia and eastward to the Pacific. (Their interests overlapped in Alaska, which the United States bought from Russia in 1867.) The integration of these great land masses depended mainly on communications and, in both, transcontinental railway ines were vital links. In great contrast British territories overseas are very scattered. The links depended this time on the steamship. Shipping routes became vital to Britain, and so did depots and strategic defensive points along them. The farthermost parts of the empire are linked by a great number of islands; some very small, but all essential in holding together the empire during its formative period. British overseas possessions are complex in another way. Some of the territories were formerly comparatively empty lands in temperate zones which could be settled by British people. These have developed modes of life similar to those in the mother country, and have attained complete sovereignty: they are the Commonwealth countries, Canada, Australia and New Zealand. Other territories lay in the tropics, already thickly peopled, but exploited by comparatively few white people for exotic raw materials. Such colonies and protectorates, the majority in Africa, are now emerging as new states.

Compared with the diversity of the British overseas possessions, the states of the U.S.A. are remarkably uniform; because in their organisation and basic culture they are all derived from a common stem. On the other hand, the U.S.S.R. covers an amazing complexity which is reflected in its organisation. Ideally its republics are based on major ethnic groups, but the largest republics also have within them territories—usually much less developed—which have less autonomy. The whole is also linked in one intricate economic system.

So-called empires or federations are not the only kind of political grouping, though they have the greatest cohesion. Military and economic ties can be entered into by any group of states which may then identify themselves as having common aims. With the exception of Canada, the states of the Western hemisphere have certain interests in common which they discuss as members of the Pan-American Union. N.A.T.O. is a military/economic union which spans the Atlantic. Inside Europe there have been marked trends towards common economic aims in the European Steel Community, the European Common Market and the European Free Trade Area.

These alliances constantly change and remind us that territorial expansion is not the only way in which one state may influence another. A political geographer should be aware of economic and ideological influences which tend to break down the seemingly rigid boundaries of the political map.

SUGGESTIONS FOR FURTHER READING

A. BARNETT: *The Human Species* (Penguin), 1961.
C. COON: *History of Mankind* (Cape), 1962.
R. FIRTH: *Human Types* (Nelson), 1960.
A. F. MOODIE: *Geography behind Politics* (Hutchinson), 1961.
J. R. V. PRESCOTT: *Geography of State Policies* (Hutchinson), 1968.
D. E. SOPHER: *Geography of Religion* (Prentice-Hall), 1967.
H. W. WEIGERT and others: *Principles of Political Geography* (Appleton), New York, 1957.

Chapter 4

MOVEMENTS OF MANKIND

4.1 FORCED AND VOLUNTARY MOVEMENTS

There are several ways in which movement of people can be classified in order to discuss what is a very complex picture. Classes may overlap or their edges may be blurred, but it is necessary to clarify the issues even at the expense of generalising and simplifying. One way is to distinguish the type and length of migration, whether it is a temporary or rhythmic and recurrent movement, whether it is short or long, whether it is confined within the bounds of one country, or international or intercontinental. Another way is to classify the motives, whether a movement is forced or voluntary, whether impelled by idealistic or economic reasons, whether for conquest or colonisation. The second is more complex, but without going too deeply into the underlying motives, for these are often confused, it is useful to distinguish the involuntary movements from the voluntary, and then to discuss various forms of voluntary migration.

The compulsory movement of people is always bound up with tragic highlights in man's history: the slave trade, wars and mass persecution and violent social readjustments to political changes. These are considerable movements involving at least tens of thousands and at most several million human beings: and their results, reflected in all aspects of human geography, have often been proportionately even greater than the mass movements themselves would suggest.

The slave trade certainly produced mass movements. The main source of those slaves who left Africa between the 15th and 19th century was a strip of its west coast about 6,400 km/ 4,000 miles in length but only up to 160 km/100 miles deep. Here, from the Senegal to the Congo, from the Slave Coast, Gold Coast and Ivory Coast, Portugal began shipping slaves in 1442. At first the trade involved only hundreds every years but during the 16th century between 10,000 and 12,000 slaves were being sold annually in Lisbon alone. The settling of the New World opened up new markets. The Papal Bull of 1493 gave Portugal the slave-producing region, but it was Spain who needed them in the Americas, and their contracts were extended to the Dutch, who began trading in 1640, the French (1701) and Britain (1713). By the late 18th century the West Indies were absorbing 50,000 negro slaves a year, and between 1680 and 1786, about 1 million went here alone. As a trade, slavery petered out in the 19th century, England abolishing it in 1807 and her possessions in 1834, but in the three hundred years or so of trading many millions had crossed the Atlantic. Estimates of the number imported into the New World vary from 5 million to 15 million, but this does not include all those who were uprooted or involved. The death rate aboard slaving vessels was usually 15 per cent to 20 per cent, and on some it was 50 per cent. Millions, too, must have died before they reached the coast of Africa, either through ill treatment, fighting or disease. One estimate of Africa's loss is as high as 50 million. Movement of people apart, the result of this enforced migration on the human geography of parts of South America, the West Indies and the southern United States was fundamental: and its imprint on the landscape is indelible.

The only comparable movements in modern times have been those connected with large-scale warfare. Wars have always involved upheaval, more particularly in the regions where they have been waged, but never on the scale of the Second World War. The First World War involved the displacement of about 6 million people, the second, about 60 million, almost all involuntary. Some people were forced to move to avoid political and religious persecution–even long before the war. Millions were moved in the forced transference of ethnic minorities, millions more in evacuation and flight from battle-fronts. Forced labour movements and deportation accounted for more millions, and subsequent resettlement involved still further movement. A million Poles and Jews were deported by Germany during the war, another million by Russia, who also moved a large number of Germans from the Volga to the Far

Eastern Province. The population of Europe was in constant flux during the war, from the Volga to Paris, and the end of the war was followed by no less marked movements of refugees. The Federal German Republic absorbed 8 million refugees from East Germany after 1945, and the Soviet Zone another 4 million from east of the Oder. It is not merely shifting populations and changing patterns which is implied in this, but vital changes in human resources, in land use, in human geography.

Some think that transference of population is the best means of solving minority problems. If neighbouring states are unhappy about the presence of large minorities of neighbours, exchange may be a solution. After the Turko-Greek war of 1921, 350,000 Turks were moved to Turkey from Greece and 1,200,000 Greeks went to their own country from Turkey. Transfer on a much greater scale followed the partition of India, where approximately 6 million Hindus left Pakistan and an almost equal number of Moslems left India, though large minorities remain in both countries.

One of the most tragic upheavals in Europe – the persecution of the Jews – had repercussions in the Middle East. Even during the inter-war period, the small trickle of Jews to Palestine was swollen by periodic persecution, in the mid-20's by 35,000 Polish and Russian Jews, in 1935 by 64,000 German Jews. Immediately before the war, Britain, as the mandatory power in Palestine, restricted the number of migrants to 12,000 a year. Immediately after the war the figures rose, and during the first six months of the existence of the new state of Israel in 1948, over 100,000 Jews moved in. But again partition was followed by uprooting and displacement. Jordan found herself responsible for 400,000 Arabs, Syria for 85,000 and Lebanon for 100,000, while 200,000 were crowded on the Gaza strip, the responsibility mainly of U.N.O.

Forced movements of people, then, have played no small part in population changes. But in modern times they are small compared with voluntary movements. Again it is necessary to qualify the kind of movements which will be discussed here. We will be concerned with movements between states, and particularly between continents. Movements within states, and more especially movements from country to town, involve less distance, though they are sometimes complex in character, but they also differ fundamentally from the others because the migrants remain within a familiar cultural context. Movement within Britain rarely brings language problems or political and economic changes, social customs, ideology, institutions are understood, adjustments are few and easily made. It is very different for an Italian peasant who suddenly lands in Boston—or, for that matter, for one of the Pilgrim Fathers when he set foot in New England: the environment is new, strange, overwhelming or challenging: breaks with the past have been made and adaptations to the new must be faced. To the first Europeans in the New World there remained only an echo of the past in their place names—New England, New France, New York, New Orleans, New Amsterdam—and the emphasis was on the new. Extension of European culture though North America was, the environment which challenged the culture was strange, and became more strange as movement went westward.

In any consideration of migration in the last two centuries the trans-Atlantic movement holds the stage, followed to a lesser extent by the peopling of Australia and New Zealand. That it deserves this prominence is shown when we consider briefly migrations from other countries which are significant enough to figure in statistics.

The number of Chinese in neighbouring states is quite considerable. There were in 1951, for example, 2,615,000 in Malaya, accounting for 44·7 per cent of the population: and there their position as merchants makes them an important factor in the economic and political life of that country. There are about 2,500,000 in Siam (14·4 per cent of the population), Indo-China has a further 850,000 (3·1 per cent), Burma 300,000 (1·8 per cent) and the Philippines 120,000 (0·6 per cent). There are few elsewhere. There are two points which emerge: (a) that however important Chinese may be in those countries in which they form a large minority, the total (under 8·5 million) is a very small migration from China's vast population; (b) secondly, their movement has been almost entirely within south-east Asia, within a whole environmental/cultural complex with which they are familiar. It is true that restrictions on the entry of Chinese into North America and Australia does not allow us to judge whether they would have moved in large numbers to new environments, but most Chinese think highly of their links with China and are most reluctant to cut ties of family and of land. Such a strongly familial society makes migrating difficult: many Chinese, their families at home in China, think of themselves as temporary rather than permanent settlers.

To some extent the same could be said of the Japanese, for although they successfully settled Hokkaido (with over 3 million) they seem reluctant to settle elsewhere. Considering the pressure of population before the Second World War, a migration of only 1,200,000 to Formosa, Korea and Manchuria (the last 'empty' temperate grassland) was trifling. Again restrictions by other nations may account for the very low figure of 25,000 other Japanese overseas, but 15,000 of these are in Brazil.

The people of the Indian sub-continent have always moved freely in south-east Asia, as religious, cultural and artistic traits testify, but generally in very small numbers. In modern times it is their movement to Africa which alone is worth mentioning, again as an element in the African population; for the total – of not much more than half a million – is infinitesimal in relation to India's population. But the 150,000 in Natal are significant, as are the 281,000 in Mauritius: and again because of their role as merchants, so are the 40,000 in Kenya, the 30,000 in Uganda, and the 23,000 in Tanganyika.

4.2 MOVEMENTS TO THE NEW WORLD

All these figures become very insignificant in face of the greatest movement of all – the modern exodus from Europe to the New World. After the first tentative foothold in the New World in the 16th century, by French, Spanish, Portuguese and English, settlement proceeded apace, backed by a steady stream of migrants from west and north Europe. In North America the colonists welcomed the newcomers who both helped to take the brunt of the Indian menace and made possible the westward expansion which was a feature of American life until the late 19th century. But the stream became a flood at the beginning of the last century, and what can only be termed as a mass migration into North America is a feature of post-Napoleonic times. This mass movement reached its first peak in the United States in the period 1845-54, when about 3 million people entered the country: and their impact must be measured against the population of the United States as it was then–i.e. about 20 million. Immigration reached a second and greater peak in the 1880's and a third and yet greater peak in the first decade of this century. During the period 1800-1924 about 60 million people crossed the Atlantic (perhaps one in six made the return journey), and of these about 36 million went to the United States. During this period Britain lost about 17 million in emigration, Italy 9·5 million, Germany 4·5, Spain 4, Russia 2, Portugal 1·5, Sweden 1, and many countries less than that. What lay behind such a movement?

There were very many causes. Motives must have seemed different to many–for this is a movement of individuals and families–but the largest single factor in the background was the great increase in population in European countries, the rate of which increased with the 19th century as the death rate fell and before the birth rate became stabilised. In the 18th century and early 19th century farming in many European countries was being reorganised, enclosure reached a new peak and there was much consolidation. There was an exodus which was only partly taken up by the industrial revolution and urbanisation: cheap and even free land must have been a great temptation to many who saw only the depravity of industrial town life. The industrial revolution also meant the displacement of artisans who sought their fortunes elsewhere. Most immigrants felt either that they were being squeezed out by pressure of numbers or that their chances of economic betterment lay in the New World. These masses were always augmented by those who went from religious or ideological motives, and who saw in the New World empty lands where there seemed to be room for everyone to build his own Utopia.

The first phase in migration to the United States, 1815–60, saw an easing in many European countries on the controls which were formerly exercised over emigration, and later migrations were encouraged. In this earlier period migrants used small vessels, many of them vessels whose return cargo of manufactured goods was so much smaller than the bulky imports of timber and cotton. Many left from ports scattered throughout western Britain—there were more than fifty ports in England and Wales and Scotland which were used by migrants. Low though the fares may seem (one could go from Liverpool to New York in the 1840's for just over £3), they represented a considerable sum to those whose only choice was to emigrate. Indeed during the Irish famines of 1845–50 the majority of those who left Ireland were small farmers who were suffering much less than the majority of the population who could not afford the passage and died by the thousand. Nor were conditions pleasant on the crowded, ill-ventilated small timber vessels. Passengers brought their own food, being supplied with no more than room to lie and an often inadequate supply of water. The voyage was long, one to three months: people died, babies were born, and if disease touched a vessel the effects were pitiful. Sometimes, as during a ship's fever epidemic in 1847, or during outbreaks of cholera, the death rate went over 10 per cent, and thousands died every year on the crossing.

The second phase was marked by radical changes in transport which were already becoming apparent in the 1850's. The coming of steam revolutionised the voyage and dispelled its perils. As late as 1856, 96·4 per cent went by sail. By 1873, an even bigger percentage than this went by steam, in larger vessels which could guarantee to cross the Atlantic in ten days or so. In the same period communications on land were revolutionised. The little ports lost their trade, and migrants now assembled in a few large ports—Liverpool was the gathering point in Britain, for example. This ease of movement might account for a slight shift eastward of places of origin in Europe, though the newer areas were often grain-producing regions, now being hit by foreign grain. This second phase, reaching a peak in

1882, and accounting for about 10 million people, was still dominated by north and west Europeans.

These first two phases can be regarded as constituting the 'old migration'. In the 'new', which dominated the third phase, 1890–1914, there were marked changes. 1890 is not, of course, a sharp boundary, for the new migration began a little before, and the old certainly continued, but the 15 million people who made up the third phase were dominated by people from Austria-Hungary, Italy, Russia, Greece, Rumania and Turkey. This was the south and east European movement. In the peak year 1882 there were 988,000 migrants, of whom 87 per cent came from north and west Europe and only 13 per cent from south and east. But in the 1907 peak of 1,285,000, only 9·3 per cent came from north and west, and 90·7 per cent came from south and east. Some of the implications of this will be dealt with later, but it is worth noting that the peak of emigration in Europe came later in those countries where the industrial revolution came later and where restrictions on movement were lifted much later than in the early migrant countries. Similar motives account for much of the movement during all the three phases, but the later movements were swallowed up more by the growing industry of the United States than by her farm lands, with the rather paradoxical situation that many southern and eastern Europeans of peasant stock found themselves in New York, Boston, and the industrial cities of the north-east.

It is worth noting very briefly the destination of the immigrants in the United States. Generalising, it can be said that the distribution and density of most of the old migrants and their descendants coincide with that of the entire population of the United States with the exception of the southern states, whose peculiar economic and social system, the tradition of negro labour, and, during the last century, comparative lack of industry, seem to have been unattractive to all immigrants. There are some regions of ethnic concentrations such as the relatively great number of Scandinavians in the Wisconsin–Minnesota area, the Pennsylvania Dutch (German), or the Welsh communities in upper New York state and east Pennsylvania. New migrants have been absorbed almost entirely by industry and

F

are markedly concentrated in the north-east, and particularly in the cities. Today many are found even in the west coast cities: the transition from rural peasantry to city proletariat is one of the great peculiarities of the migrant story.

Migration to the New World came to an abrupt end in 1914, and when it was resumed its character was very different. But it should be remembered that the great period of mass migration had also witnessed the peopling of Canada, South America, South Africa and Australia and New Zealand, though the countries of origin were much more restricted.

4.3 INTERNATIONAL AND INTRASTATE MOVEMENTS

For many reasons the period of unhindered movement ended in 1914. Immediately after the First World War the United States began legislation to limit entry, many fearing the indiscriminate entry would soon swamp Americans themselves. Entry was then restricted to about 154,000, and each European country was given a quota of this total, depending on the percentage of the people from that country in the population of the United States in the 1890 census. This was clearly discriminating, for it gave high quotas to the old migrants and very small ones to the new. It was a measure to preserve the Anglo-Saxon or north-west European origins of Americans. In fact the old migration was drying up—Britain did not fill her quota—but the new was still clamouring for entry. Until recently, therefore, the migrant stream was small, particularly from Asia and southern and eastern Europe. But the quota system ended in 1968, to be replaced by a preference scheme based partly on the skill the immigrants could offer. To some extent the new scheme, too, was preferential, relatives of citizens of the United States being preferred; and a limit was still kept on the total intake of migrants. The result was that in 1969 nearly 360,000 migrants entered the United States, 114,000 from Europe, 72,000 from Asia and 89,000 from Latin America, most of the last coming from the Caribbean. From Europe, Italy sent the largest number (27,000), followed by Ireland (17,000), Portugal (16,000), Great Britain (15,000) and Germany (10,000). In addition the United

States accepted refugees and displaced perrsons. 9,000 of these came from Europe, mainly from eastern European states.

Australia also controls immigration. Many motives combine to exclude all those who endanger the standard of living or do not belong to the main cultural and racial stock. Excluding the aboriginal population, Australia is still predominantly British, and the White Australian Policy, the Federal Immigration Restitution Act of 1901, aimed at 'racial purity', economic wellbeing and social homogeneity ('The desire that we should be one people, and remain one people, without the admixture of other races'). Yet British immigration to Australia remains small, the population is still only 11.5 million and estimates of a possible population vary from 30 million to 60 million.

Nine and a half million of Australia's population is Australian-born: nearly one million were born in the United Kingdom. The 'British' character of the population is in no danger of being challenged. But the trickle of migrants has included Europeans of various nationalities for several decades. The population includes a quarter of a million Italians, 140,000 Greeks, 100,000 Germans and 100,000 Poles. In spite of the tremendous pressure of population in neighbouring South-East Asia, the number of Asians in Australia is insignificant.

South America, in particular Argentina and Brazil, has had a small but constant stream of European migrants. This increased markedly during the 'quota' period in the United States, when the number of Italian migrants, for example, swelled considerably: in 1950 nearly 80,000 went to Argentina compared with 9,000 to the United States. Spanish migrants also figure largely in the movement to South America.

The only Asian country with significant immigration is Israel. There was a steady trickle between 1919 and 1947, totalling nearly half a million Jews, mainly from eastern Europe. This increased considerably after the state of Israel was created, reaching a peak in the 1950s. Since 1948, 1,300,000 have entered the country, a massive addition to a small population. By 1969 the annual figure had dropped to 25,000.

The population structure of migrating groups is hardly ever

normal. Emigrants from Italy in 1950 provide an example of this. In that year nearly twice as many males migrated as females (92,152/48,052), and the great majority was in the age groups 15–45. This is the structure one would expect, and it does have an effect both on the residual population and on the population of the receiving state. It represents the movement of a labour force, but the relatively fewer number of women also means that intermarriage in the country of reception might aid eventual assimilation.

The intercontinental movements which have been discussed so far are the most spectacular and the ones which give rise to most problems, but migrations can also be international or intrastate. A very large number of Italians live in southern France; Paris has a large Polish population; and movement from Ireland to Britain is continuous. Interstate movement is even more widespread. This involves none of the risks, maladjustments, officialdom or even cost of international migration. Within a state there are normally no language barriers, no 'racial', no religious barriers; adjustments need not be great. The motive is almost always self-betterment.

Movement in the British Isles is dominated by two aspects: (a) migration shows continuing rural depopulation and increasing urbanisation, and (b) the distal and highland regions are losing to the south-east and particularly to the metropolitan region. This last is a region of absorption, as opposed to the regions of dispersion in the south-west, upland Wales, northern England and upland Scotland. The Glasgow–Edinburgh region shows a gain, as does the west Midland region, but London is the greatest recipient.

The attraction of the conurbations – large city clusters – in Britain for the people of Wales, Scotland and Ireland is shown in the table which appears at the top of the facing page, of the number and percentage of persons in the conurbations who were born in those three countries (1951).

To a certain degree, proximity has an effect on the regional distribution. Merseyside has a great attraction for the people of North Wales, and to a less extent south-east Lancashire, and the west Midlands have a similar attraction for South Wales.

	Wales		Scotland		Ireland	
	Population	Percentage	Population	Percentage	Population	Percentage
Greater London	151,971	1·8	140,564	1·7	202,638	2·4
South-east Lancashire	24,571	1·0	26,202	1·1	43,288	1·8
West Midlands	41,161	1·8	20,466	0·9	45,722	2·1
West Yorkshire	7,876	0·4	16,952	1·0	16,719	1·0
Merseyside	30,890	2·2	18,283	1·3	32,231	2·3
Tyneside	2,965	0·4	18,258	2·2	4,858	0·6
Total	259,434		240,725		345,456	

Movement from Wales to west Yorkshire is limited and is very small to Tyneside. In the same way these last two conurbations have much less attraction for immigrating Irish, but a high proportion of Scots go to Tyneside. But the greatest attraction is, of course, London. Over 59 per cent of those born in Wales and now living in the six conurbations live in London, over 58 per cent of Scots, and over 59 per cent of the Irish.

In the United States internal migration has not long been dissociated from the western movement of people which gradually filled in the continental area between 1800 and 1900. Officially the frontier disappeared in 1890, but migrations continued as the east lost population and the west became increasingly populous, as negroes from the southern states moved to northern towns, or, as in special instances, people left areas like the Dust Bowl following agricultural 'over-production'. One American writer sees migration in the United States as having been of four main types: (a) the pioneer spread from the east beyond the Alleghenies, a movement of farmers dependent on waggons; (b) the deepening and concentration of population in industrial sectors, an era served more by railways; (c) the rise of urbanisation, particularly with the increase in administration and services; and lastly (d) the movement out from cities into suburbs and commuting area, dependent on the motor car. The most striking of these is probably the urban movement. In 1790, when the population of the United States was under 4 million, 94·9 per cent was rural, 5·1 per cent urban; in 1890, with a population of 63 million, 64·9 per cent was rural, 35·1 per cent urban; in 1960, with a population of over 195 million, only 30·0 per cent was rural, 70·0 per cent being urban.

There seems little doubt that cities owe their growths mainly to migration. Certainly in the last century, when Western European cities grew so rapidly, this was the case, for natural increase was small until the gradual diminution of mortality rates. Although health improvement and other factors have considerably altered this general situation, birth rates are still lower in cities and it is still doubtful whether cities do perpetuate themselves. It is probable that after stabilising itself a city population tends to decline, so the importance of continuing migration is marked.

4.4 'LAWS' OF MIGRATION

Can any generalisations be made about movements in general?

'Laws' of migration were formulated by Ravenstein in 1889; and although we question the desirability of using the word 'law', his generalisations are worth considering. The most important are:

1. That most migrants travel short distances. The stress laid in this chapter on intercontinental movement should not be allowed to hide the fact that internal migration is a continuing feature of all modern states, and that the total movement – although it is not a mass movement – is immense.

2. That migrant population is absorbed in zones, i.e. the short movement from an area will leave a vacuum which will be filled by movement from beyond. This leads to a sort of wave movement.

3. Each movement has a compensating movement in the opposite direction. Net migration from country to town is the

balance of movement into the town over movement from the town into the country.

4. Migrations over longer distances tend to go directly to the larger centres, particularly to metropolitan cities.

These generalisations still hold to some extent, but the greatest modification is the disproportionate part played today by the fourth generalisation following the greater ease of movement in this century. For example, many Italian migrants in the United States settle on the west coast: having made the Atlantic crossing, the continental crossing is comparatively easy. Moreover the big city seems to be increasing its attraction at the expense of smaller towns, and communications of all kinds – radio, television, newspapers, as well as transport – ease the steps from distant rural areas to central metropolis.

Finally a word must be said on the implications of migration generally. If its only result were the redistribution of mankind it would be of interest as an agent of population change. But it is more than that, because where men move they take with them their culture – their technology, ideas, ways of life. Looked at very broadly the whole of North America, for instance, is an expression of the transference of a north-west European urban and industrial civilisation across the Atlantic. The whole complex relationship of man, society and habitat which is laboriously worked out and patterned on one part of the earth's surface is transferred to another. This is the history of mankind. The plough–seed complex became perfected in the Middle East before it transformed Europe's landscape: rice irrigation spread throughout Monsoon Asia: the Spaniards introduced the sheep and horse to North America and in so doing revolutionised the economy of the Navajo and vastly increased the potential of that of the Plains Indians. A *new* England appeared on the forested shores of north-east North America, its villages not very different from those of the old, but contrasting greatly in economy and society from the Indian culture it replaced: while north of the St. Lawrence the subtle differences of European culture are still reflected in Quebec's linear villages, strip farms, French language and Roman Catholic religion. Dutch barn in Pennsylvania and neo-classic portico in Virginia are both expressions of an extension of the Old World in the New.

But the new countries of the world–the Americas and Australia–were, after all, only new to Europeans. Patterns of life had been arrived at there long before, based on simpler economics and more primitive cultures. These have been replaced. Man has come to terms with the habitat in a new way, and the resulting landscapes are an expression of this, an expression of his ability to move freely and to take with him all those elements of culture with which he adapts himself to his environment.

SUGGESTIONS FOR FURTHER READING

A. T. BOUSCAREN: *International Migrations since 1945* (Praeger), New York, 1963.

M. A. JONES: *American Immigration* (University of Chicago Press), 1960.

D. R. TAFT and R. ROBBINS: *International Migrations* (Ronald Press), New York, 1955.

C. WILLATS and M. NEWSON: 'Geographical Patterns of Population Change', *Geographical Journal*, CXIX (4), 1953.

Chapter 5

OBTAINING FOOD

Man's primary activity is getting food. This was so when there was little to differentiate him from his ape-like forebears. It is still so, though his food-getting activities have by now transformed so much of the surface of the earth. In the intervening period he has learnt to cultivate plants and to domesticate animals, to control river systems and floods, even to create new land by reclamation from the sea: and as a result he has so increased in numbers that it seems that only new techniques in production and distribution will alleviate the hunger which still haunts so many men, women and children today.

In the earliest stages of his development man was a gatherer and hunter, in a way no better off than his animal contemporaries until he invented weapons which helped in the hunt and discovered the advantages of fire. Relics of this stage remain to remind us of the kind of existence which must once have been universal. Such peoples as the Bushmen, the Semang and Sakai of the Malaya peninsula, the Australian aborigines and the Tierra del Fuegans, still exist on gathering and hunting. This kind of economy implies a simplicity, particularly of equipment: but we should not underestimate the technical advantages of such inventions as the boomerang or the blowpipe or the simple bow; nor forget the knowledge of location of wild animals and plants which these people possess, and the know-how which is passed on from person to person and from generation to generation.

When we consider that in addition to the simpler cultures named above, the Eskimo and the fishers of the north-west coast of America for example are also food gatherers and hunters, we realise that we are not dealing solely with technically simple cultures. The Athapascan Indian has 176 implements concerned solely with getting food, 23 for fishing alone, including 15 kinds of fishing line. The Eskimo has a high level of material culture. His winter and spring sealing alternates with summer caribou hunting. The tools of his trade – the umiak and kyak, the harpoon with detachable head, the s-bow – are marvels of ingenuity: and nothing is more ingenious than the way in which he adapts himself to a very unfavourable environment by means of tailored clothing, bone sun-goggles, snow shoes, sleds, and above all, the igloo.

No less interesting is the way in which the Plains Indians' life revolved around their food supply, the bison, before their economy and society were swept away by the advancing frontier of the second half of the 19th century. Although over-dependence on one food is a sure way of periodically going hungry, the Indians evolved a considerably complex material culture on the use of this one animal. The hide of a bison with hair retained made thick winter clothing, and shields; with hair removed, thinned and softened, it made shirts, leggings, moccasins, tents, bags and the envelope-like 'parfleche' in which dried food was carried; strips of hide made ropes and lines; the hair stuffed pillows and saddles and was used in decoration; sinews made thread and string; hooves, glue; horns, utensils; and bones, tools.

We need not, therefore, think of gathering and hunting as a simple primitive stage only: it developed in its own right as a complete economy which could lead to complex cultures and to a thorough exploitation of the environment. Nor must we think of this economy as being exclusively concerned with hunting, fishing and gathering. The dog, which is probably the most common and the earliest of the domesticated animals, figures prominently in the lives of hunters: and the Plains Indians had even one cultivated plant, namely tobacco. Gathering berries, roots and nuts nearly always supplemented hunting, and small game relieved the vegetable diet of people – like the Paiute of California – who were predominantly gatherers. In the same way an element of gathering and hunting has remained in most other economies, even in our own; though blackberry-picking and foxhunting no longer bear much relationship to our food supply.

One thing is common to all gatherers and hunters: their task is a constant one. Storage is difficult and food is eaten when it is obtained. There is no security, no leisure, indeed there is no permanent home; for families and larger groups must move with the game, must find new areas for collecting. The Plains Indian followed the bison herd, his home, the tipi, easily packed on the travois. As a hunter his range and efficiency were greatly increased when he learnt to tame and ride the horses which had been introduced by the Spaniards in Mexico, and which had wandered in a wild state into the plains. They became the Indian's greatest asset and increased his mobility. Eskimos move seasonally, and so do the coast fishers of British Columbia who exploit the sea in summer, and the rivers in winter. Of all these groups the fishers are the nearest to being sedentary.

The food-collecting stage occupied long millennia in the history of mankind. Man was omnivorous and very mobile, but his entire energy was expended on food. The cultural advances he had already made were important–he had discovered the use of fire, he had invented tools and he could communicate his ideas by speech. These three–fire, tools and speech–have been called the tripod of culture. But radical though they were, these advances were to serve mankind until comparatively recent times. Nor did they make any great impression on the landscape or, with the exception of fire, change the earth's surface to any degree. The part played by fire in landscape change is only gradually being realised, but if some of it was due to human activity it was done unwittingly and not with a purpose. For the most part palaeolithic and mesolithic men took what the environment offered and had no great powers to alter it. These early gatherers and hunters were very thinly spread on the earth's surface: and very widely spread, for the relicts of such communities are at the farthest parts of the earth from those regions where fundamental changes in methods of obtaining food were to take place in neolithic times.

Looked at historically, or prehistorically, the next stage for which abundant evidence is available is that of communities of farmers, well established in the Middle East by about 5000 years B.C. The change from food gathering to food producing is fundamental in man's history. It has been called a revolution, a word which does signify the radical nature of the change but which might give a wrong impression concerning the time which the process took. The innovations which were involved probably took a very long time, both to be discovered or invented and to be adopted by the society and thus begin the transformation of the economy. They certainly initiated very far-reaching changes in the environment.

Before discussing these changes, let us remind ourselves of the general features of a simple farming community in the old world. This description will necessarily ignore intermediate steps which may have preceded farming of this kind and those simpler forms of cultivation which are still found in many tropical regions. It will emphasise rather the magnitude of the changes which were implied in even the earliest farming communities: and these must be realised before we deal with the possible ways in which they came about. The Cochin Indians of the Malabar coast are rice cultivators. They occupy land which was once clothed in dense forests, but there are now no more than remnants of this, for it has been replaced by intensive cultivation. This in turn feeds a very dense population, averaging over 380 per sq km on the coastal plain: for two or even three crops of rice are possible on the richer lands. The Cochin Indian tills his land with a simple wooden plough which has an iron point but no mould board or wheel or coulter: its long beam is yoked to water buffalo or oxen; during cultivation manure is scattered on the fields to increase their fertility. The seedlings as they grow are regularly watered, raised tanks controlling flooding of the fields. Where one crop only of rice is grown, millet, pulses or oil seeds are cultivated, providing food for the period during which the paddy crop is still growing. Scattered among the houses are gardens and orchards, the larger of which have breadfruit, mango, bananas and other trees: most gardens have pumpkins, melons, yams, taro and roots and vegetables. The coconut is the most important orchard crop. In addition to water buffalo, livestock include cattle, sheep, goats, and in some Syrian Christian communities, pigs. Fishing, both in the sea and in rivers, supplements the food supply. Most of the people live in villages, in a great variety of houses reflecting the complexity of the economic and social strata which are part of the Indian caste system: for in addition to those producing food these communities have a high proportion of artisans of all kinds.

Compared with food-gathering cultures, the fundamentally new elements in this picture are many and obvious. The original forest cover has been stripped away, thus radically altering the landscape. Wild species of plants have been replaced by cultivated species; not one, but many, including cereals, root crops and vegetables; several species of domesticated animals have been introduced, and contribute to the economy – providing draught power, dairy produce or meat. Even more remarkable is the combining of these features in a complete agricultural complex, for the plough is drawn by a domestic animal, and the manure is ploughed back into the earth. Fishing is still an element in the economy, but collecting is now organised into gardens or orchards. The sedentary village is a new feature, and so is the great density of population. The ability to grow so much food, much of which can be stored, has given rise to a large stable population, which in turn provides the pool of labour so necessary in paddy irrigation. In addition to this it is apparent that there is surplus enough to support groups of people who are not concerned in food getting – artisans, priests and princely castes. All this emphasises the great differences between food collecting and food producing.

The fundamental elements in this method of obtaining food – cultivation, domestication, irrigation – were all present in those early communities in the Middle East 7,000 years ago. Their introduction is sometimes known as the neolithic revolution, because it is linked with a technical change in the way man fashioned his implements. In palaeolithic and mesolithic times tools had been made almost entirely from chipped flints, and though some of these chipped implements reached a very high degree of competence – and beauty – they were very inferior to the polished stone implements which superseded them in neolithic times. The polished stone axe had a fine edge which surpassed all previous cutting tools, and this enabled neolithic man to cut down trees for extending cultivation: these axes also helped make pens for animals and shelters for human beings. But even more fundamental was the way in which man began now to exploit the vegetable and animal kingdoms by a series of discoveries. The assumption that gatherers became cultivators and hunters became herders, and that a combination of both gave rise to a mixed farming of the kind just described, is over-simplified and probably erroneous. The earliest farming communities which archaeology has revealed in Egypt and Mesopotamia are already complex, that is, cultivation and domestication exist together, even before they have supplanted the gathering economy which preceded them. Our familiarity with mixed farming could blind us to the magnitude of the changes it implies. Farming in Egypt in 5000 B.C., based on wheat and barley cultivations, was in many ways much nearer to 20th-century farming than to the economies which preceded it.

Where and how did cultivation first arise? It is reasonable to suppose that the distribution of wild varieties of plants like wheat and barley limited the area within which cultivation first took place. Wild forms of two kinds of wheat are known. Emmer wheat was the primary prehistoric grain and a wild form is known in Syria, Israel, Iraq and Iran. Einkorn, which was cultivated later than emmer wheat, is found in a wild form in Anatolia, north Syria and the Balkans. No wild form is known of bread wheat, which is thought to be a hybrid of emmer and einkorn or emmer and a wild grass. Wild varieties of barley are found from Russian Turkestan to Tunisia. Thus the possible area of the origin of cereal cultivation is centred on the Middle East. An orthodox view of the process of cultivation is that mesolithic food gatherers were already using the seeds of these grasses in their wild form. Until recently the Paiute of the basins of North America practised a similar economy, for their food supply depended largely on seeds of numerous grasses: indeed the parallel may be even closer to prehistoric Egypt, because snow-fed streams from the mountains were diverted by the Paiute to irrigate patches of land and thus give more luxuriant grass growth. In Egypt it is assumed that increasing desiccation, lack of game and a reduction in the amount of wild grasses would have stimulated cultivation on the periodically flooded valley floor. Thus, according to Daryl Ford, irrigation agriculture may not be a specialised form of rainy season cultivation, adapted to arid lands, but the forerunner of all cereal cultivation: it certainly demanded no clearing of forests, no weeding, and merely called for extending the flooded area to increase the food supply.

Whatever prompted these new discoveries – and we shall see in a moment that there are points of view other than that given above – the wild forms of cereals could not have been adapted to cultivation simply at man's own whim. Wild plants cannot be reaped: they scatter their seeds too quickly. Paiute women must keep on beating the seeds from the grasses before they are lost: they are gatherers, not reapers. Men could only progress from this stage when they found a variety of the cereal which was a mutant, i.e. an unexpected and unexplained form, in which the pod did not burst open of its own accord: this means that time could be spent in reaping before the seeds needed to be used or stored. Cultivation must have come after a very long period of trial and error, or as an imitation of other forms of planting.

It is very likely that oats and rye, both of which can grow outside the cultivation limits of wheat and barley, were not discovered independently, but were first found as weeds in crops of the latter. Rye is still a 'nuisance' crop of this kind in a wheat field in Asia Minor. When approaching the cultivation limit of wheat, a poor year which will kill off the wheat will allow rye to survive and so give a different cereal crop. The same is true of oats, which will grow in areas too cold and too wet for wheat. A similar argument has been put forward for the cultivation of dry rice (grown on drier ground with a fair rainfall), as distinct from irrigated rice. The latter is presumed to be a substitution in south-east Asia of western cereals, but using the same techniques as wheat cultivation, the ideas having spread into first the Indus basin and then beyond.

Millets and sorghums are cereals which give small grains much less nourishing than wheat and barley, but which can be grown in areas too tropical for wheat and barley and too dry for rice. The first millets were probably cultivated within the same region as wheat and barley and were known in early Egypt: one species was very widespread in prehistoric times and found in the Mediterranean in classical times. Similar grasses and sorghums are very widespread in Africa, both in forest lands and on drier grasslands.

One thing is fairly certain, that the cultivation of the cereals in the Old World was part of one complex farming process, tied to plough cultivation, which probably spread from a centre somewhere in the Middle East to the whole of the Old World within the climatic limit of such cereals.

The second great innovation of the neolithic food producers of the Middle East was the domestication of animals: it was closely tied up with cultivation. Archaeologically domestication appears first within the area of the earliest cultivation of cereals. Within a comparatively short period in the early stages of agriculture in the Middle East most of the animals which proved to be useful to man had been domesticated. For whereas cultivation has been applied to innumerable species of plants, comparatively very few animals have been successfully domesticated. As far as food supplies are concerned the important ones are: cattle, sheep, pigs, goats, reindeer; horses and camels and yaks are more important as beasts of burden, as are the llama and alpaca. The dog was of particular use to the hunter and probably preceded all these. The conditions necessary for domestication include these: gregariousness for herd animals, docility, a liking for man, love of comfort and the ability to breed in captivity. Few animals fulfil all the conditions. Several birds have proved important both for food supply – eggs and meat – and feathers: they are, chicken, duck, goose, pigeon, peacock and turkey.

Domesticated animals have been useful to man in several ways, not only as a direct supply of meat, but for their milk (particularly sheep, reindeer, oxen and goats), as beasts of burden (the pig being the exception), and even in providing

fibres, furs, skins and feathers. Selection has led to great specialisation (e.g. cattle are bred for meat or milk, sheep for meat
or wool), and to an enormous variety within species: dogs become selected for scenting, pointing, retrieving, burrowing,
herding sheep, herding cattle, producing a great variety of
breeds. But even so, the number of species domesticated remains
very small, and many are found in the earliest farming communities on the Nile. It looks as if man exhausted the possibilities of domestication almost as soon as he discovered the art.

Some scholars are satisfied that all the conditions for domestication were met in the Nile valley in prehistoric times, when
desiccation led to the concentration of men and animals on a
shrinking water supply. According to Childe, 'this enforced
juxtaposition produced the symbiosis we know as domestication'. Again the Middle East is certainly a focal point in the
wide region where wild species of domesticated animals occur
and within which domestication could have originated. Wild
ox had a very wide distribution in Europe and south-west Asia,
and it is difficult to decide whether south-west Asia or the Nile
was the original centre of its domestication. Domestic sheep are
derived from the mouflon, which survives in Iran and Anatolia
and in southern Europe until recently, and the urial, found
over a wide area of south-west Asia. There is no evidence of
wild sheep in North Africa. Mesopotamian sheep seemed to
have been derived from the mouflon, Nile sheep from the urial.
The goat almost always accompanies the sheep in Asia and
Africa, and again it is derived from a wild species which had
a wide distribution in southern Europe and south-west Asia.
There is much in common between areas of wild cereals and
useful wild animals.

The horse and the camel are comparative latecomers. The
first evidence for the former dates to about 2000 B.C.: derived
from the steppes, the horse was particularly associated with
riding. The camel came even later; both dromedary and
bactrian were desert animals.

It is difficult to assess how purely economic were the factors
underlying domestication, for again we are probably over-
influenced by our own use of these animals. Some writers have

been so impressed by the extent to which cattle were connected with ritual in the ancient civilisations of Egypt and Mesopotamia that they have eliminated the economic motive from the earliest stages of domestication. Ritual does not demand full domestication, but milking implies advanced domestication, i.e. this economic use came long after the first stages of domestication and could have played no part in its origin.

Some interesting features of the distribution of domesticated animals will be brought to light if we look for a moment at some of the features of pastoralism among simpler cultures of today, i.e. economies which depend almost entirely on domesticated animals. The first striking feature is that pastoralism is characteristic of the Old World, not of the New. The Navajo sheep herders of the south-western United States adopted this economy from the Spaniards who introduced both sheep and horse into the New World. The llama and alpaca, one the domesticated form of the guanaco, the other of the vicuna, both part of the pre-Columbian civilisation of the Andes, were kept for transport and wool respectively, rarely for food. The New World's only other contribution to domestication are the turkey and the guinea-pig, for the dog, companion to the hunter, probably came in from Asia with man himself.

The second striking feature is the way in which the dominant animals of the simple pastoralist economies are zoned and bear a very strong relationship with habitat. The reindeer herding of arctic and sub-arctic Asia gives way to horse breeding in the steppes: this in turn gives way to the camel in the dry zone and to cattle in the sub-tropical belts of savanna. These breeds are not, of course, exclusive: the camel herders have horses, the horse herders sheep and goats, and the cattle herders sheep and goats: most of them have dogs, but these do not enter into the economy except sometimes as an ancillary, e.g. in herding other animals. Even more significant is the presence of some animals in apparently unsuitable habitats. Such is the horse in Badawin country. The Badawin's camel is central in his economy, and this animal's adaptations to the arid Arabian interior are obvious, particularly its ability to go unwatered for a week even in parched land, and for much longer if it has access to grass:

moreover its hump is a reserve of fat on which it can live for days even when pastures disappear. The camel supplies food and valuable material, and can be exchanged at oasis villages for goods of all kinds. In spite of this the horse is more highly prized than the camel; yet it serves little economic purpose and is, in this habitat, most exacting in its requirements and demands great care. Horses are useful in raiding, but otherwise they would seem to be a liability. Nevertheless they are often accorded more care than the Badawin's own family, for the horse is a symbol of status in the community. So divorced is such a symbol from the rigid requirements of desert life that the features sought for in a thoroughbred are purely arbitrary, e.g. a white horse is the most prized, although the camel's colouring is a reminder that this is not nature's choice.

The seemingly illogical occurs again and again. The Masai cattle herders who live on the rim of the African rift valley south of the equator must not slaughter their own cattle, although they may eat the meat when the cattle die. Even more curious is the fact that of the two types of cattle in this economy, the longhorn is much more highly valued than the shorthorn, although the latter yields twice as much milk as the former. Again the purely economic function is overlaid by a social one. The Masai herd sheep and goats as well as cattle and are the most purely pastoral people in Africa: outside Masai territory in East Africa generally, cultivation increases in importance, but as it does so, so the ceremonial and religious significance of cattle increases, and are even more divorced from the food supply.

Another characteristic of simple pastoralism is nomadism. Pastoralists are tied to the needs of their herds. If pasture is sparse then the human population is scant, and what pasture there is must be sought by constant movement. Reindeer in the cold wastes of northern Siberia need about four square miles of country per head to find sufficient food to live. However much man supplements his own food supply by fishing, this means an extremely sparse population, continually on the move. The Badawin illustrate seasonal movement well, moving from winter pastures to spring in a clockwise direction from the Hamad to

the fringes of the Nefud, and to the oasis settlements of agriculturalists in summer when drought is at its height. The horse
herders of the central basins of Asia had a similar seasonal
migration over great stretches of territory. A modified version
of this kind of movement is transhumance, which once characterised very many peasant communities in Europe and is still
found in Norway and Switzerland for example. The cattle are
taken in summer to the high pastures (called 'alp' in Switzerland, 'saeter' in Norway, 'shieling' in Scotland), where women-
folk often have temporary huts and see to the milking: in
autumn the cattle return to the valley floor for wintering. There
are relicts of the practice in Britain: the name 'booley' in
Ireland and 'hafod' (literally 'summer house') in Wales is evidence of how widespread this practice used to be.

The distribution of pastoral economies in the Old World
seems to suggest that it is best developed in areas beyond those
where cultivation could easily be carried on. This implies that
it did not originate as a totally separate economy, tied exclusively to domestication, and contributing to mixed farming
only when it came into contact with cultivation. It is, rather,
a specialised, and later, offshoot of an originally mixed farming
economy, specifically adapted to certain marginal conditions.
Its partial dependence on fixed agricultural communities in the
dry lands, as among the Badawin, suggests this: and at the
other extreme, so does the emphasis on hunting among the
northern Reindeer herders, where domestication is only partial.
The technique of milking seems to peter out as one goes away
from the centres of ancient civilisation towards the north and
east.

The views on the origin and spread of agriculture which were
mentioned previously in this chapter are widely accepted,
though it is obvious that a great many gaps in our knowledge
have been bridged by assumptions and conjecture, and simple
economies today have had to supply clues to the unknown past.
Deep though our archaeological record goes it does not throw
sufficient light on these problems outside the ancient civilisations of the Middle East. Many would prefer not to entertain
alternative ideas on the origin of agriculture because the evid-

ence which is available points fairly at the conclusions already
discussed. Different theories have been put forward, however,
which deserve consideration: more particularly one by an
American geographer, Carl Sauer; and although there is no
archaeological evidence yet for his theories his ideas are original
and more comprehensive than the orthodox views and help us
to see new possibilities in this very complex problem. Sauer
refutes three premises which are assumed above: (i) It is
assumed that sedentary life follows the change from food
gathering to food producing. Sauer claims that there must have
been sedentary communities *before* the change could come
about. (ii) That hunger and the need for food was an incentive
to the change. Sauer argues that the change could only arise
from a surplus, that it took place in a region of plenty, not one
of difficulty. (iii) That agriculture began in the semi-arid belt
of grassland. Sauer would locate it in forest lands which are still
the home of the simplest agriculturalists (e.g. the Boro of
Amazonia). Grassland, says Sauer, is the most difficult of all
habitats to cultivate: even the 19th-century American was
temporarily halted when he came to the great plains. Sauer
accepts the Middle East origin of cereal cultivation and, with
modifications, its subsequent spread into Europe and North
Africa and India. He emphasises more than previous writers
the specialisation into pastoralism on the periphery. There is
a parallel expansion of maize cultivation from Central America
into the north as far as the St. Lawrence. But cereal cultivation
might well be an advanced economy, and the origin of agriculture might belong to quite a different and earlier complex–to
the planting economies of the tropical forests. Sauer's cradle of
agriculture is south-east Asia. Here, he claims, would be found
groups of mesolithic fishers, the only kind of collecting economy
which leads to *sedentary* communities. These would be river
communities in a land of great physical and organic diversity,
a region of plenty.

The basis of the kind of agriculture which Sauer postulates
is the planting of tubers with a digging stick. Tuberous plants
multiply asexually, i.e. tubers are broken off the main root and
planted, in the way we plant potatoes. The Boro of Amazonia

provide a good example of what is implied in this type of economy. The preliminary work involves clearing a parcel of forest land, and this is done by burning the larger trees and clearing the ground with stone axes. The main agricultural implement is the digging stick, with which the ground is roughly prepared, a hole made in it, and the tubers of manioc of a cultivated variety planted. Yams and sweet potatoes are similarly planted. After two or three harvests the ground is exhausted and a new area of forest must be cleared. In Africa, tubers—more particularly yams—are the mainstay of the hoe cultivators of the west. Yam and taro and sweet potatoes are basic foods, too, in Oceania. Here, other foods besides these starchy ones are often found in association, such as bananas and plantains, and fishing is an important supplement to the diet.

Sauer claims that this type of agriculture, dependent on the digging stick and hoe, and on the planting of tubers, is essentially simpler and older than planting cereal by scattering seeds on ploughed land. It is a forest culture derived from a mesolithic base of a sedentary fishing economy. There is an interesting link with domestication: these economies possess only the dog, pig, fowl and duck, all household animals and sharply differentiated from the herd animals which were mentioned above and which belong to the seed complex. The household animals certainly had only a small economic value and fall more readily into the category of pets. They are traditionally farmyard animals and, as Sauer points out, are still the responsibility of the women, who could both run the household and keep an eye on them. Women also played a large part in planting and collecting—though men did the clearing and supplemented the food with fishing and hunting.

The idea of two agricultural complexes, planting tubers and sowing seeds, helps to clarify the issues and to provide a more complete picture. The next step depends on logical argument, rather than on evidence. This is the development of the seed/herd complex from the planting economy. The clearest link is seen in the New World where digging stick technique and forest clearing is basic to the production of a cereal, maize. But instead of planting a tuber, seeds are dropped into the holes made by the digging stick. With the maize were planted beans and squashes, and this complex–and the agricultural methods which went with it–spread through the forest lands of North America as far as the St. Lawrence. It was spread by cereal farmers who were fundamentally planters. The plough was never a part of this complex. Did the same thing happen in the Old World coupled with a change of technique and the invention of the plough? Could dry rice have been a weed in a southeast Asian planting complex? Sauer points out that irrigation, which characterises the early stages of cereal cultivation, needs an organisational not a technological revolution, and this could only come from an advanced culture which was already sedentary and agricultural. With the exception of the reindeer, domesticated herd animals go with seed cultivation, and Sauer thinks that their origin had nothing to do with economy; pastoralism has developed peripherally to cultivation as a special adaptation to marginal conditions.

5.2 WORLD FOOD DEMANDS

We now turn to a more comprehensive picture of man's primary activities today. How is agriculture meeting the demands of the world's vast and increasing population? The basic demand, as always, is to sustain life, though often at a very low level. The energy and heat needed to keep the body going come from fats and carbohydrates, particularly from the latter in the form of starches and sugars. These last are found in the cereals and tuberous roots whose origins were discussed above, and these are the fundamental foodstuffs. Indeed the needs of most of the world's peoples may be summed up by the two phrases 'daily bread' and 'a cup of rice'; 64% of the world's population have a diet which includes 80% to 90% of cereal or potato. Only 10 % of the world population, living in the United States, the United Kingdom, New Zealand, Sweden and Switzerland, eat less than 40% of their food in this form.

About 4% of the entire land surface of the earth is used for growing cereals. Wheat covers about 1.6 million ha/4 million acres, rice and corn both over 0.8/2, oats 0.5/1.3, barley and rye over one each. Following its first cultivation in prehistoric times in the Middle East, wheat growing expanded along the Mediterranean and northward into Europe. The Mediterranean climate was ideal for its growth, but this was only the first stage in its expansion. The next was reached when it was found that spring wheat could be substituted for winter wheat, i.e. the more rigorous winters of Europe beyond the Mediterranean could be overcome by spring planting and the area of wheat cultivation was thus greatly increased. Even this extension was small compared with post-industrial revolution expansion, when the great natural grasslands were exploited in North and South America, Russia and Australia. The inventions which made this possible included railways to penetrate these lands, to take in men and take out grain, and all the technical innovations which opened up the prairies. The latest expansion of all follows seed selection, hybridisation and artificial crosses, all of which have enabled the limits of wheat growing to be pushed farther outwards.

Wheat cultivation was carried from the Old World to the New. Corn (maize) went in the opposite direction. In pre-Columbian times its cultivation had already shown a remarkable spread from its origin in Central America. Its world distribution is now wider even than wheat, though North America still produces more than half the world total and has the highest yields. Its spread is largely the result of the many varieties which have been cultivated and their adaptability to varying climatic conditions; but the main areas of corn growing are in the United States, Argentina, south-east Europe, Java and China. Much of it is used for animal feed and is converted into meat.

Rice is the world's other great grain crop, concentrated in monsoon Asia and peculiarly suited to that climate. Between 90 per cent and 95 per cent of the world crop is found here, nearly a third in China and a fifth in India. More will be said later about the intensive kind of farming which characterises the rice area and its dependence on an abundance of human labour. But it should be noted here that as rice is grown under irrigation conditions its limits today are not so strictly physical as cultural, i.e. it extends within that area which has similar technological and demographic characteristics.

The other important group of carbohydrate foods includes the tubers. The yam is a staple food in West Africa. Its cultivation depends on the digging stick and the hoe; and the fairly rapid exhaustion of the land which it entails has given rise to shifting agriculture, i.e. after two or three seasons a patch of land is abandoned and a new one cleared. There are several varieties of yams giving succeeding harvests: but they can also be stored. In Oceania the taro is more important than the yam: it is smaller, but has an all the year round growth. It must be eaten when gathered. This is a characteristic of hot belt agriculture which makes it nearer to gathering as an economy: ripening may be very rapid and decay even more so. Fruits must also be eaten almost immediately. In temperate climates in mid-latitudes storing over the non-productive season is extensive; not only in cereals, but in fruit, which can be dried, or made into wines and beverages.

The potato is a native of the New World. It was a staple food in the Andean cultures, for maize was cultivated at a lower level while potatoes thrived above 3000 m/10,000 ft. In the late 16th century it was brought to Europe where its production is now very wide. Germany and Poland are second and third to Russia as producers: indeed the potato has the reputation of having opened up the great north European plain.

All these vegetable foods are staples in world diet. But at all levels there are other ingredients in the diet to give some balance of proteins, the tissue-making substances. This is often provided by pulses, but more particularly by meat, eggs, fish and milk. The body also needs other foods which supply more than the needs of energy and tissue replacement. It needs protective foods such as vitamins, often contained in fruit and vegetables. And in advanced economies food production goes one step farther in providing exotic foods which give pleasure but are not essential to life. These last needs—or desires—have stimulated the exploitation of tropical countries for the benefit of temperate countries; have in fact opened up much of the plantation areas of today. At first these demands were for small quantities of 'luxury' foods: spices from the East Indies and West Africa, tea from India, coffee from Arabia and chocolate or cocoa from the New World. These food habits were ushered in with the beginning of Europe's overseas empires in the 16th and 17th century. The demand for sugar arose in the same way. Sugar is one of the cheapest commodities, but paradoxically its use is directly related to the higher standards of living.

The demands of the body, the varying eating habits of different societies, the range of men's techniques, the climatic and organic needs of a great variety of plants, the economics of demand and supply and the problems of distribution: all these combine to give the distributional patterns of agricultural practice which must now be examined (Fig. 5.1).

5.3 TYPES OF FARMING

Occidental. Western farming belongs essentially to mid-latitudes, from 30° N. to 60° N., and, with exceptions, 30° S. to 40° S. It is found in Europe with the exception of northern Scandinavia and extends well into Siberian Russia: it characterises North America east of the great plains and is found again on the west coast: the tip of South Africa, parts of Chile, Argentina and Brazil and south-west Australia all have similar groups of economies.

The first and simplest economy in this group is subsistence farming, i.e. the economy of more or less self-sufficing communities who market the minimum of their produce. This must have been once the most widespread economy, characterising peasant communities. Its distribution is now more restricted, typifying parts of Eastern Europe in particular. The dominant crop is a cereal, and small numbers of livestock, a few cattle, pigs and fowl, are usually kept. The essential element is the lack of surplus.

General mixed farming is a development from this. The most important land use is arable; wheat, oats, barley, rye in Europe and maize in the United States are the dominant crops. Oats is a fodder crop and is also used in rotation systems: indeed many arable crops are used as fodder and enter the market as meat, milk and eggs. Farms are medium in size. In

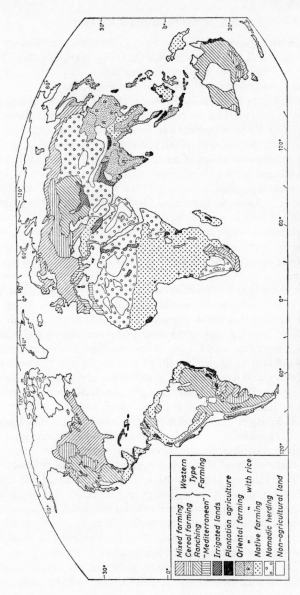

Mixed farming		Western
Cereal farming		Type
Ranching		Farming
"Mediterranean"		
Irrigated lands		
Plantation agriculture		
Oriental farming		
Oriental farming with rice		
Native farming		
Nomadic herding		
Non-agricultural land		

Fig. 5.1. Distribution of major agricultural economies.

Britain they average about 30 ha/75 acres, and the density of farming population is consequently fairly high. Much of the produce enters the market for exchange and small towns therefore characterise these rural communities.

Dairying, as a specialised form of mixed farming, coincides with the great urban belts of the West, more particularly in north-west Europe, north-east America and south-east Australia. Milk is the predominant produce and the link with the needs of dense clusters of towns is obvious. Dairying is also predominant in countries where pasture is good, such as Ireland, Wisconsin, Michigan and Minnesota: elsewhere oats and hay are dominant fodder crops. Cattle are specially-bred dairy breeds, such as Jerseys, Guernseys or Holsteins. In addition to milk dairying belts produce butter and cheese, both these, but cheese in particular, being storable and able to withstand transport and distance from cities. Farms are again moderate in size.

The third major type of Western farming is composed of the great grain belts of the world. The distribution of wheat is less a function of ideal physical conditions than a result of economic sorting out processes. For example, the United States, Argentine and Canada come very low in the ranking of yields (16/15/14 hl per ha/18, 17 and 16 bushels per acre respectively) and compare very unfavourably with European countries such as Denmark (41/46), the U.K. and Germany (30/33). But the problem is not so much getting the best out of the land as getting the most with the least number of workers. The characteristic of the great grain belts is extensive, not intensive, farming: fields are large enough for extreme mechanisation, and this means a great amount of production with little human labour. With such granaries available after the 1860's, the countries of Europe could not hope to compete, whatever their yield, and Denmark, for example, went over to dairy farming. Sparse population, then, is typical of these lands of immense farms. Only occasional towns break the landscape: these are the collecting points, strung along the railways which cross the North America prairie; they are an essential prerequisite of such development, and notable only for their immense silos. Practically the entire crop is for use *outside* the production area: the farming is wholly commercial.

There are other specialised types of Western farming. Truck farming, the growing of vegetables and fruit, depends on an urban market, and more particularly on the quick transport of the produce to the market. In this way arose such unique areas as the Aroostock Valley in Maine, producing potatoes only, or the Imperial Valley of California with its lettuce and melons.

The last specialised type of Western farming to be considered is one which takes us back to pastoralism, i.e. commercial grazing. It is the extension of pastoralism into the New World in the last hundred years or so which is particularly interesting, although similar developments have taken place in Asiatic Russia. This is no subsistence economy but a highly commercialised farming which exploits the world's grasslands beyond those regions where grain farming is successful, i.e. in the high grasslands of North America, in South America, South Africa and Australasia. There are, of course, radical differences between commercial grazing and pastoral nomadism. It is often linked with crop growing for winter feeding, either by dry farming or by irrigation, so its dependence on natural grass is not exclusive. And its settlement, though extremely sparse, is fixed, not nomadic. Transhumance is sometimes practised, e.g. in Montana, where the high pastures are used in summer only, and the cattle are hay fed for five winter months in the ranches: in spring they move to the foothills and in June they are again in the Rocky Mountain pastures. The landscape is one of immense ranges, fenced by barbed wire, and scattered ranches. A single ranch in Oklahoma, specialising in cattle for breeding, is 3,640 ha/9,000 acres. Only 280 ha/700 acres are not in native grass, and most of this produces sorghum and alfalfa. Railways and roads are essential in this economy, for the produce – cattle, sheep, wool – must be shipped to the packing and consuming centres which are outside the ranching regions. The markets for the western plains of the United States are in the eastern states; those for Australia and New Zealand, which demand meat, wool and dairy produce, are the other side of the world. Nor could this kind of economy flourish until Western technology had devised fast steam transport and refrigeration. These grazing areas together with the world's commercial grain belts are the lightly peopled food-producing areas without which the Western industrial states could never hope to survive.

Oriental farming. Turning from Western exploitation of temperate grasslands to south-east Asia, our scales need drastic revision, both in size, age and populations. We turn from extensive farming to intensive, from very recent innovations to age-long processes, from the world of machines to the world of men, from sparse population to teeming millions, from cash crops to bare subsistence.

So intense is cultivation in some regions, such as the alluvial lowlands of China, that the pattern is reminiscent of market gardening: it has been called 'the agriculture of pigmies'. In the overcrowded lands of south-east Asia the only aim is to feed the greatest number of mouths on a restricted amount of land. Two elements alone are abundant: time and labour. All else must be conserved. The labour needed in paddy rice cultivation is immense: land must be graded, channels cut, rivers bunded, the earth tilled and hillsides terraced to create steps of level land – always for more paddy. But the labour is abundant: enough indeed for multi-cropping. And the fertility of the soil is renewed, not only by the water itself in the form of silt, but by wastes of all kind, human and animal. Capital is slender: equipment is primitive – the hoe and simple plough suffice – but skill is considerable and plentiful.

There is little animal husbandry in this economy. China's Great Wall was the divide between the desert and the sown, between pastoral and agricultural economies. Oxen or buffalo help draw the plough, but poultry and pigs are the only other common domesticated animals – the pigs especially being able to live on scraps unfit for human beings.

The pattern of farming has changed little for four thousand years or more: this economy is a measure of man's ability to adapt himself to the environment. The pressure on the land has certainly increased, as the average size of farms shows (1·3 ha/3·3 acres in China): and this has been aggravated by fragmentation of holdings, for even the smallest farms may be in from 5 to 10 strips, and the dividing baulks themselves are wasteful and make the application of any technique other than that of the hoe or simple plough impossible. Another wasteful element shows the close association of the Chinese with the soil: these are the grave mounds which sometimes appear as a rash on the landscape, and collectively eat up 2 per cent of the available land.

The villages, towns and cities are a reminder of the civilisation which was built on this economy, which spread from an origin in north China to the whole of monsoon Asia, and which took with it this very distinctive technology and pattern of agriculture. It will take a considerable time for the radical social changes of the last fifteen years to transform such a pattern.

Irrigation farming. The controlled use of water has enabled man to transform some of the most difficult environments to the most fruitful, more particularly in the hot dry belts of the earth. The early civilisations of the Near East were based on such control. There was no essential difference between the prehistoric control of water on the Nile and that of paddy rice cultivation today. It was flood irrigation, in which water was admitted to a series of basins during the time the river was in flood, and allowed to stand there before emptying back into the river bed when the level subsided. This meant a seasonal regime, for the flood begins in June, reaches a peak in September and subsides gradually to December. Growth cycles and agriculture were tied to the river regime. Wheat was the staple crop–cotton, for example, could not be grown because it demands spring water. The kind of control which allowed watering at all seasons had to wait for the technology of the industrial revolution, and this initiated an immense step forward in irrigation agriculture. The first barrage which stored back water which could be used at all seasons was built a century ago in the Nile delta, by European engineers. The real impetus came in the 1880's and 1890's when the Asswan dam created a reservoir which opened up 200,000 ha/500,000 acres for perennial irrigation. The increase in Egypt's population is one pointer to the success of these methods, from $2\frac{1}{2}$ million in

1821 to 7 million in 1900 to 20 million in 1950. And the introduction of cotton as a cash crop lifted the economy from its old subsistence level.

Between 1870 and 1900 immense schemes initiated by the West began to transform the Punjab from a region of marginal farming, in which pastoral nomadism was a dominant element, into a prosperous region. The waters of the five rivers have been distributed in the doab regions and the great Sukkur dam on the Indus has transformed the Sind. 4 million ha/10 million acres have been opened up to food crops (2·5/6 of them to wheat), and over 0·8/2 million to cotton. A shifting population has become settled in planned townships, and increased enormously. In 1891 the district of Jhelum in the Punjab had five towns, in 1931 it had thirteen. Its population in 1891 was 60,000; in 1951, 2,150,000. The density of population increased during that period from 7 to 240 per sq km/17 to 612 per square mile. These are projects which, incidentally, are threatened because the headwaters of the Punjab rivers are in Kashmir and others have an international boundary with India along them. For irrigation agriculture control of the entire river system is essential to ensure supplies of water.

The great schemes of Egypt and the Punjab, developments of the last 80 years or so, are obviously something which Western society has imposed. They need immense skill, the culmination of a technological revolution born in Europe, and they need the capital investment which only industrial and commercial countries can supply. They have transformed the indigenous economy. They have also transformed semi-arid areas in the New World, where capital has been similarly applied. Vast schemes have aided the development of New South Wales, Victoria and South Australia. And possibly the most spectacular schemes are those which irrigate the dry lands of the United States. The possibilities of irrigation there were shown by the Mormons in Utah in 1847, but it was another half century before the bigger schemes were initiated. Although 5 per cent of United States agriculture is dependent on irrigation, little of this is basic except for some animal foodstuffs like alfalfa. A considerable amount of dairying is found in addition to alfalfa in the mountain states, but most of the irrigated land produces exotic and luxury foods, the extras which vary the American diet, and consequently they are highly specialised in fruit or vegetables. North American irrigation emphasises another point. It is there coupled with the control of the water resources of entire river basins, and is linked with power supplies. Hydro-electric generating plants are as important as irrigation. But these vast projects involve great capital, so much so, that a high percentage of the cost is borne by the federal government.

Plantation agriculture. However capable mid-latitude countries have been in developing their basic food resources, they have often had to look elsewhere for those small vegetable foods which have added zest to their lives and enabled them to preserve and flavour their foods. Spices were never carried in great quantities, but they formed the wealth first of the Arabian caravans, then of the Venetian trade routes, and of Portuguese fleets, before other Western European countries shared in this commerce. Sub-tropical empires were based on the need for cinnamon, cloves, pepper, opium. Some of the later luxuries, particularly the beverages introduced to Europe in the 17th century, tea, coffee and cocoa, and tobacco, led to the increased interest of the West in the tropics.

Plantation agriculture marked the invasion of Western needs and methods into the tropical world. Its produce is usually required in comparatively small quantities, but most of the crops have fairly rigid requirements: so plantation agriculture is scattered in small favoured patches, further tied to the coast because accessibility is of overriding importance. Other require-ments are an ample labour supply, capital and relative political stability under which continued production is guaranteed. The contrast between this purely commercial exploitation, geared to the needs of high standards of living in temperate countries, and the subsistence agriculture or gathering economies indi-genous to the tropics is dramatic; as sharp as the contrast be-tween the stands of single species which typify plantations and the myriad species which characterise the tropical forests.

The outstanding features of plantation agriculture are, there-fore, the emphasis on a restricted number of crops, and its

H

large-scale commercial basis. A little food may be grown for local consumption, but even this may be imported. Even where pressure on the land is considerable plantations may dominate, as in Cuba, where more than half the land is under sugar, part only being under maize, fruit and grass. There is little subsistence and the abundant labour is mainly concerned with the cash crop.

Plantation land very often bites into virgin forest. For example, in the coffee-growing area of Brazil the more interior plantations have a large proportion of land under forest. A forested valley side is cleared from the ridge top, and coffee plants will occupy a growing area towards the valley bottom. Within the planted area there is no diversification other than an orchard and an area of cane sugar used as animal fodder. The owner of such a plantation will often be a city man, but his interests here lie in pushing forward the frontier of farming. It is cheaper and easier to expand his plantation into forest than to maintain the older plantations, and for that reason only the best land – usually the ridge tops – are used, amounting to 20 per cent or so of the total, and less than half even in the intensely cropped areas.

Java provides one of the few examples where plantation agriculture has been integrated with indigenous subsistence agriculture in a land where population pressure has been intense for a considerable time. Fortunately sugar and tobacco production alone demand conditions similar to rice production, and these are the only produce which seriously clash with local needs: the Dutch formerly regulated the area under these particular plantation crops. Tea, coffee, rubber and cinchona flourish best in formerly unproductive areas. Their requirements vary so that tea, for example, needing more than 500 mm/20 in of rain in the four driest months, is found on slopes between 600 m/2,000 ft and 2,000 m/6,500 ft in the west: coffee, demanding a dry season, is concentrated on the lower slopes in the east. Cinchona demands conditions similar to those of tea, but rubber is found in east and west.

To sum up, plantations have always been geared to outside needs and demanded outside skills, techniques and capital.

They show the imprint of advanced temperate cultures on the underdeveloped world of the tropics.

SUGGESTIONS FOR FURTHER READING

V. G. CHILDE: *What Happened in History* (Penguin Books), 1942.

R. DUMONT: *Types of Rural Economy* (Methuen), 1957.

C. D. FORDE: *Habitat, Economy and Society* (Methuen), 1957.

H. F. GREGOR: *Geography of Agriculture* (Prentice Hall), 1970.

C. SAUER: *Agricultural Origins and Dispersal* (American Geographical Society), New York, 1952.

T. SHANIN: *Peasants and Peasant Societies* (Penguin), 1971.

L. J. SYMONS: *Agricultural Geography* (Bell), 1966.

D. WHITTLESEY: 'Major Agricultural Regions' (in *Wagner and Mikesell*, op. cit.).

Chapter 6

FARMS AND VILLAGES

6.1 BUILDING MATERIALS

Although man's primary need is food, the need for protection and shelter is also fundamental and universal: protection from the harsher elements of his habitat: from extremes of heat and cold, rain and snow: from animals of all kinds from carnivores to insects: and from the hostile activities of his own kind. At the most primitive level a fire has often served some of these needs, and sometimes been the only protection; but even the simpler societies have met wind and weather with varying degrees of complexity by devising clothing and shelters.

Clothing lies outside our scope. Not so man's means of sheltering himself, of building houses and so creating distinctive features of our landscape. The study of settlements, culminating in towns and cities, is central in human geography. In this chapter we will be concerned with rural settlement only.

Using the term 'shelter' in the widest sense, at the lower end of the scale men have been satisfied with mere wind breaks, temporary screens facing the wind and protecting them and their fire. In the arctic a temporary bank of snow might serve the same purpose. Through degrees of elaboration men have devised simple conical huts, tents, log dwellings, mud and brick and stone structures; some to house families, others to serve society in a wider sense. Differences in the form and function of these structures vary so enormously that they could be the subject of another book.

Man has always tended to build with the materials nearest to hand. In the forested lands of the world – in Europe, Russia, North America – timber is the dominant material. Even in regions such as Western Europe, where the all-timber house is unusual, timber has often been the traditional frame filled with brick or plaster. With the settlement of North America, what more natural than that use should be made of the timber which had to be cleared even before crops could be grown? The 'log cabin' which has its antecedents in Northern Europe has left its mark. Today about 90 per cent of the houses in the United States are of timber. One of the great difficulties facing farmers who, a hundred years ago, were trying to settle the great plains, was the lack of timber: they were moving into a strange environment and many of their first houses were sod huts.

Reeds and grasses have, of course, been extensively used elsewhere. In Africa, in semi-arid regions, stunted bush and scrub, though excellent for the protective ringing of man and beast, could never carry a heavy structure, and here the dominant forms are small conical or rounded huts, thatched with grasses. In yet more arid regions the earth itself serves. Clayey soil can be moulded; it hardens in the sun, or can be baked; and it can be mixed with straw and small stones. Going north from the equator in Africa, mud walls replace timber and thorn, and soon that is replaced by mud and bricks. Bricks are an invention of the arid zone, and their smallness has meant great flexibility of form. Corbelling and arching were the fundamental techniques which resulted, and Europe, in particular, made great use of bricks.

Stone is another basic building material. Limestones and sandstones have offered the greatest possibilities, but granite, slate, schists, marble, have all been extensively used. Among the simpler peoples the Hopi of New Mexico use sandstone in their pueblos. In Europe the low cottages of the west coasts are of stone—in the west of Ireland, for example, where trees are sometimes rare, or on the bare Welsh hillsides, where slates, grits and granites tie the houses firmly to the habitat. The warmer softer limestone links the Cotswold cottages to their background quite as effectively. Stone has come into its own in particular in monumental buildings, which are outside our present scope, in Egyptian or Mayan pyramids, Greek and Indian temples, Gothic cathedrals, renaissance palaces.

In Europe materials are varied and often mixed, though dominance of one or another will often give a region a very distinctive character, as do the timber frame, half-timbered houses of the Welsh border, the red bricks of the Midlands, the Cotswold limestone. An entire house is rarely of one material, and there are further regional variations in roofing, for example, such as thatch (which may be of rye or wheat or even sods, all depending on the region), wooden pantiles, ceramic tiles or slates.

The connection is usually very close because building material is bulky, heavy and difficult to transport. There is more movement today in building material, but before the railway era anomalies were few. Monumental and sacred architecture sometimes called for exotic materials. Pembroke- shire stone went into the making of Stonehenge; and as stone has seemed more fitting for monumental architecture through- out history, this often was an exception to simple regional relationships. Great use has always been made of certain limestones, marbles and granites.

Many other features of house construction proclaim the habitat. The inward-looking courtyard-houses of the hot zones have dark, cool interiors; the steep roofs of temperate and tropical zones are water-sheds in heavy rain; the tying and pegging of thatch and the cementing of slates in Ireland and Wales respectively are reminders of strong, persistent winds. All these elements reflect the very close relationship between house and habitat which must constantly be kept in mind.

6.2 SITE, PATTERN AND DISTRIBUTION OF SETTLEMENT

Before dealing in any detail with settlement we should per- haps distinguish between several elements in the study. There is a tendency to think of settlement as one problem, and con- sequently ingenuity is taxed in trying to balance the great variety of factors, both in the physical environment and in the cultural, which have a bearing on it. But it should also be remembered, that if we here distinguish three separate aspects –site, distribution and pattern–that it is purely for the con- venience of analysis and to avoid difficulties in confusing causative factors: these three are inextricably tied together.

Site is the relationship between a dwelling or a group of

dwellings and the immediate physical environment. It is a very minor feature of the landscape – part of a slope, a raised hillock, a level terrace, a south-facing aspect, proximity to a spring. Sometimes a site is peculiar to a single dwelling, sometimes to a whole village.

Pattern of settlement is the relationship of one dwelling to another, sometimes irrespective of site. The fundamental division which is usually accepted in rural settlement, dispersed or nucleated, is one of pattern. But there are very many patterns, degrees of dispersion and different forms of nucleation. Often a pattern is unrelated to site and site may have little or no bearing on pattern.

Distribution in the present context will refer to the much wider aspects of settlement. Where are the settled areas, for example, and where the unsettled? What are the limits of settlement? In many cases this is a continuation on a much bigger canvas of consideration of site. If aspect is important in site, then it can refer, for example, to a whole valley side. It has been shown that the distribution of settlement in Swiss valleys is very closely connected with aspect and the duration of sunlight. Lack of water, prolonged cold spells, extreme altitude, all are fundamental limiting elements and consequently are vital in studying distribution. One cautious note should be given here. How definite are these limiting factors? And if settlement limits vary from one period to another in the same locality, what then decides the extent of settlement and its limit? We glibly suggest 250 m/800 ft as a limit in some parts of Britain, 275 m/900 ft in another, but we should be careful to specify that these are today's limits. A map of the distribution of settled areas in Britain in the Bronze Age would soon correct any impression that settlement is of necessity a lowland feature or even that we must look for an *upward* limit. Coming to much more recent historical times, the upward limit during the Napoleonic wars was higher than it is today. Indeed a study of settlement maps over the last 150 years will show that in Wales, for example, the limit crept upward during the expansion of the rural population in the first half of the 19th century, then crept down, leaving many a field to go back to mountain pasture and many a derelict stead. Settlement distribution reminds one of a wave washing the mountain side, sometimes high, sometimes low. One can only talk of a limit as long as it is related to a specific time, realising that it is the time which determines those limits. So 'limit' means different things at different times. It is rather like the horizon. Looking out to sea from a promenade the horizon is definite enough, and it is about 5 km away from the observer. Let the observer stand on a small hillock and he looks at another horizon, now 10–15 km away. He can search the sea in vain for *the* horizon. Any horizon depends on the position of the observer; so with our limit of settlement. There is no contour which tells man he can go no farther. The limit is a reflection of society's needs and ideas at any one point of time.

The three elements, site, pattern and distribution, are obviously related, but their separation helps in our analysis. We need not be bothered with pattern when discussing limits – the distribution could be dispersed or nucleated settlement: and siting need not be important in discussing pattern. I say *need* not. It *can* be of course, if sites are so restricted and pressures so heavy that every available site is utilised. This may happen in Asian paddy rice districts: here, site and pattern are one; the latter is a result of the former. Again, if the need for defence has dictated the use of hill sites, the fact that this is a collective need, relative lack of suitable sites means that a village pattern will probably arise. But on the whole we will be dealing in this section with pattern.

Pattern of settlement has been defined as the relationship between one house or building and another, and to isolate this relationship it is a simple matter to take it off a large-scale map, by placing a dot for each building on tracing paper. But in doing this several things have to be borne in mind. First we should remember that we are abstracting the pattern from the habitat, that we are ignoring site, and that we may well have to put the pattern back into its context to arrive at any conclusions. Secondly we should know whether or not the buildings we are dealing with are houses, and if not we should know their function and allow for this. For example, a large farm complex, consisting of house, tractor sheds, granary, cattle-sheds and outhouses, might give the same pattern as a hamlet, though from every other point of view differences are fundamental and must be allowed for. In the same way a 20th-century service centre, consisting of small store, garage, post office, school and community hall, may well be confused with a hamlet in which there are none of these features. The pattern method is useful as long as we are satisfied that we are dealing with uniform social conditions, or that each unit signifies exactly the same thing. Lastly and most important of all we should be conscious of the historic depth which may be part of the settlement. Large-scale maps in Britain reveal not merely a pattern which can be explained in modern terms, but former patterns which have arisen under different circumstances and can only be explained historically. The modern pattern may be the outcome of a long period of change. There is no one explanation of a complex settlement pattern. To make a single sweeping generalisation, to explain the existing pattern even of one country, may be misleading. Meitzen, in his classic division of European settlement patterns into nucleated and dispersed, coupled this division with two fundamentally different types of society; some have suggested an explanation based on racial differences, others have explained settlement in terms of soil or the availability of water. Each 'universal' explanation has fallen down wherever it could be shown that the pattern has changed in historic times. In Guernsey, which Meitzen unhesitatingly placed in the dispersed area, late 18th-century estate maps show clearly that at that time the pattern was nucleated. The first ordnance survey maps of Ireland, drawn in the 1830's, show that much of the country – now considered a classic example of dispersed settlement – was a mass of hamlets, and dispersal was absent. 'Racial' distinctions have not changed, nor have the soils, so that answer to the pattern must be sought for in the society which produced it. Studying today's pattern is a limited exercise unless we link it with a study of development, where we may find different factors operating at different times.

6.3 OLD WORLD SETTLEMENT PATTERNS

Man is a gregarious animal whose fundamental tendency is to remain grouped, sometimes in a family, often in a clan. Theoretically one might put forward a case that the small nucleated settlement is the primary form, and that all dispersal is subsequent. Among the simpler societies the cohesion of social groups is often reflected in communal dwellings. In the Amazon valley the Boro live in large groups, many families living under the one roof of a large single house which may be 18 m long

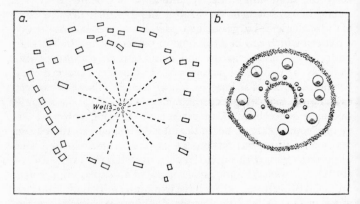

Fig. 6.1. Both the Badawin encampment (*a*) and the African kraal (*b*) are inward-looking settlements in which animals are protected overnight.

and 9 m high. Each family has its own fireplace around which personal belongings are kept and where they sleep, and sometimes these quarters are screened from each other by matting. The dwellings of the north-west coast Indians also house a number of families: but these communal houses are themselves closely grouped into a true village.

This primary urge toward nucleation is emphasised by the need for protection for man and beast. This applies to temporary as well as permanent settlement. The plan of a Badawin encampment in Arabia is of two roughly concentric circles of tents around a well. At night the animals are gathered inside this area and the spaces between tents filled with brushwood if that is possible (Fig. 6.1). The African kraal is a closed community for similar reasons. Masai huts are arranged in a circle outside which is a brushwood fence and inside which is a further penned area for cattle, sheep and goats. Zambia has fine examples of multiple kraals in which about a thousand huts form an immensely big circle. Immediately inside this is a series of a hundred or so cattle pens. Near the centre of the open space is a kraal in which the huts of the chief, his wives and retinue repeat the circular pattern.

In none of these is there a feeling of houses being packed closely together as in some villages where agriculture makes the first demand on the land. Iranian walled villages are very crowded, for there is no building at all outside the walls. Compactness reaches an extreme in southern Arabia, in the valleys of Hadhramaut, where villages form very compact blocks just above the limited cultivated land in the valley floor. In some cases the villages are made up of minor skyscrapers of 6, 7 or 8 stories. A village might consist of up to 500 such houses, and so restricted is space that new houses are built only when old ones are pulled down.

Extreme crowding is sometimes found in China where land is precious enough: the high street of a market town may well be a canal, and in some cases 50 per cent of the entire settled area is under roof (Fig. 6.2). Nor should we forget, in this context, the vast numbers of people who live over or on water. North Borneo pile villages are built over water for protection; in many Chinese delta areas there is a vast floating population, though this is largely an extension of urban rather than rural settlement.

But it is rarely that close nucleation is the product of one factor only. One cannot dissociate pressure on land from need for protection – the Iranian villages are walled – and as the need for either diminishes, nucleation may still persist, for it is a form which also reflects social cohesion, and may be found in association with specific kinds of land tenure.

Monsoon lands are predominantly village lands. Although

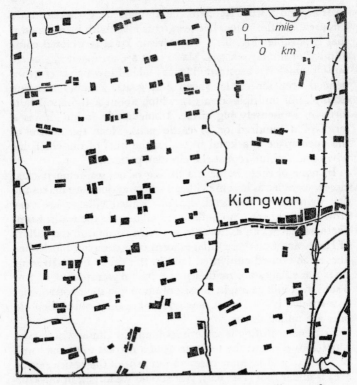

Fig. 6.2. China's lowlands have very numerous villages, often so congested that the market town's highroad is a canal, as at Kiangwan near Shanghai.

many parts of China have dispersed habitats, the majority of country folk live in villages. There is too much variety to specify a distinct form, but the elements of nucleated peasant houses surrounding a temple and a few shops, and protected by trees, are fairly common throughout. It is even more difficult to suggest how big these villages are, for they range from tiny hamlets through villages of several thousand people, and they grade imperceptibly into market towns, which are even bigger. Indeed small towns here, as elsewhere in advanced communities, must be accepted as part of the rural settlement pattern, and the pressure of population is such that they may be found at intervals as small as a mile. Traditionally such centres have also had administrative functions.

In Japan, too, villages are the rule. But again one should not think of the remainder as being exclusively of markedly nucleated village. The unincorporated hamlet, which is a common form, is no more than a loose cluster of 15 to 20 homesteads, each in its own field: and the only building other than farms might be a communal shelter house which might also house a deity. Some such hamlets on a major highway develop into small shopping centres. Site often decides the actual form of larger villages, as is often the case in irrigated lands: street villages develop along routes and compact villages are found in paddy lands. On alluvial lowlands these latter are scattered over the land, but in hillier country they are sited near the valley floors and near level land. Again villages merge into the much larger market towns; but although there are many more non-farmers here the market town is rarely differentiated into shopping area and residential. Hokkaido and its dispersed habitat is rather exceptional, for the pattern of land division and roads is geometric in this comparatively recently settled region. This is a pattern highly reminiscent of the middle west of the U.S.A. It is significant that dispersion here, and in limited areas elsewhere, is the result of very recent expansion.

Comparatively few people in India live in dispersed dwellings. Even in the Himalayan zone and hill country generally the hamlet is the main unit of settlement. In Bengal even the technically dispersed settlement makes a close pattern indeed. Elsewhere the nucleated village is supreme. Generalising about form is meaningless because each village is an untidy maze of paths and, apart from being compact, relatively formless except where a fort for defence, or alignment along a level or at a break of slope, tends to give rather more form than usual (Fig. 6.3(a)). One feature which is common to many villages on the great alluvial plains is that they often occupy mounds which are the relics of forerunners of the villages of today. Mud and sunbaked brick disintegrate easily, and new houses are built on the rubble of the old. But socially there is usually marked differentiation within Indian villages, for castes are allotted their specific localities. The market place is always near the centre of the village together with several shops, and the core of modern administrative services – post office, police and grain store. Larger villages also have mosques or temples and their schools, and several public wells. This is the predominant

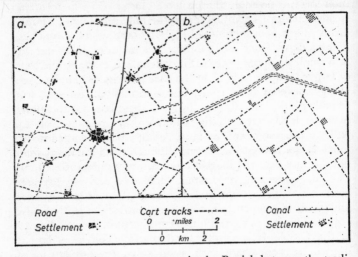

Fig. 6.3. There is a great contrast in the Punjab between the traditional haphazardly clustered villages (a), and the planned rural landscape (b) which is the result of canal irrigation.

type and seems the peak of haphazard growth. In marked contrast the colony villages of the Punjab, brought into being in the last half century since the massive irrigation projects have been initiated, are strictly planned (Fig. 6.3(b)). They are rectangular, with an open space where stands the mosque and shops: so new, so strange to India, that their impersonal pattern is emphasised by the fact that they are often numbered, not named.

One of our starting points for nucleated settlement was the African kraal. It is impossible to generalise on village or compact settlement forms for the whole of Africa, but those few studies which have been made stress again the variety of forms and the transitional nature of some of these. In one region alone in Nigeria, for example, there are closely nucleated villages, nucleated hamlets, dispersed and almost continuous settlement, ring villages and dispersed compounds. All which emerges from this is the caution not to generalise too much but to examine each settlement problem in its own setting.

Settlement patterns in Europe are at once more familiar and, perhaps because of that, more difficult to explain. There are

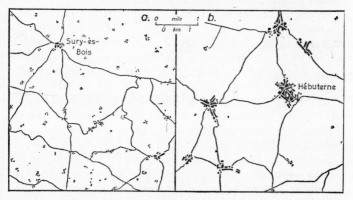

Fig. 6.4. Some regions of France have scattered rural settlement (*a*); others show marked nucleation (*b*).

scores of detailed studies, but very few which relate patterns in different countries or which suggest general tendencies. Increasing knowledge forces one to accept former generalisations, like those of Meitzen, only with innumerable qualifications, and also makes one shy of substituting new generalisations. Change has so accelerated in the last half century that what was a slowly evolving rural pattern has often been rudely shattered or so overlain with very recent accretions that a regular pattern is hard to find. It would be wrong to ignore these new additions, and very wrong to assume – without evidence – that if this could be removed one would be dealing with *the* settlement pattern. Settlement study is meaningless unless it takes into consideration the changes which time has imposed. The student looks at a stage in settlement pattern, and the core of his study is the process by which such a stage develops.

As throughout this study, the two constant elements are the two extremes – nucleated and dispersed. In France, for example, the north-east is the land of the villages, though they are found also along the Mediterranean coast and in Languedoc where defence has necessitated using certain sites (Fig. 6.4). Brittany and most of central France is the land of the dispersed farm, though the scatter of hamlets in this pattern is significant. The south and south-east is a country of mixed patterns. No simple environmental explanation is acceptable. The differences do not always coincide with water supply; for example, water supply is plentiful in the Ardenne, but settlements are nucleated: it is much more difficult to obtain in limestone areas, but here houses are dispersed. Different patterns overlap all kinds of subsoil. The nearest correlation is between villages and open-field systems of tenure; and dispersal and the greater amount of pasture in the west, where settlements are also near what arable land there is.

Similarly, in Germany there is a great variety of forms with definite regional tendencies, but the development of rural settlement in Germany is a reminder of the significance of historical sequence, for change and expansion went hand in hand, and no direct and obvious link of land and settlement is true either for all stages of settlement or for all regions (Fig. 6.5). What might well be directly descended from the original settlement patterns of the loesslands of southern Germany is still a dominant form – the irregularly clustered village on the edge of its striped arable field, meadow and pasture and woodland. This irregularly clustered grouping is called *Haufendorf*, or sometimes *Gewanndorf* after the striped pattern of the fields. The truly scattered habitat (*Einzelhof*) of today is found in the north; but this might well be a secondary pattern, the dispersal of former hamlets, small open clusters (*Drubbel*) which represented single communities. The *Drubbel* was small, often less than a dozen houses, but some which did not disperse became the

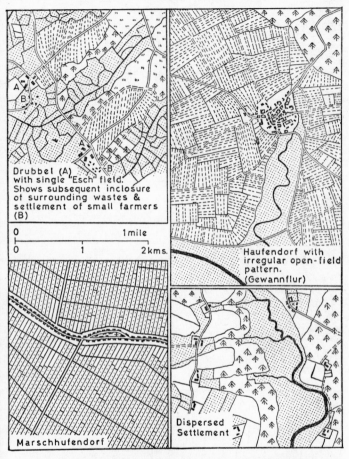

Drubbel (A)
with single "Esch" field.
Shows subsequent inclosure
of surrounding wastes &
settlement of small farmers
(B)

| 0 | | 1 mile |
| 0 | 1 | 2 kms. |

Haufendorf with
irregular open-field
pattern.
(Gewannflur)

Marschhufendorf

Dispersed
Settlement

Fig. 6.5(a). Rural settlement forms of western Germany.

nucleus of larger villages. After the 12th century the Germans colonised the lands east of the Elbe/Saale. This was not devoid of settlement, but the Slavs who thinly peopled it had few settled agricultural communities, and these were villages of irregular pattern, loose clusters of houses. The expansion into this land

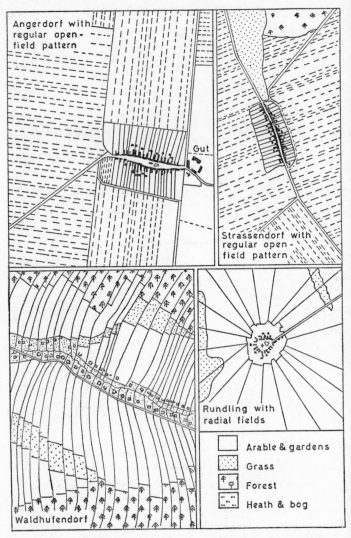

Fig. 6.5(b). Rural settlement forms of eastern Germany.

saw new forms, more formal and planned, side by side with the strip system of arable farming. The *Strassendorf* (street village) emphasised lines of communication, but less rigid was the *Angerdorf*, which leaves a lacuna of common land; most striking is the *Rundling*, as its name implies a round settlement found along the former line of contact between Germans and Slavs.

The only generalisations which can be drawn are these: that primary forms were small and loosely nucleated: that they lacked a pattern: that this is still found in hamlet-types: that

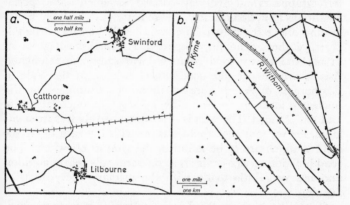

Fig. 6.6. The typical settlement pattern of lowland England is of nucleated villages with some dispersed farms between (*a*). But such innovations as drainage channels in the Fens introduce marked modifications (*b*).

dispersal is often but not invariably secondary and much of it due to change in land tenure and consolidation: that the more formal planned types are later and represent medieval expansion into comparatively new land.

We can enquire in a little more detail how such changes can come about by looking at settlement patterns in Britain. The broad division is between lowland England with a predominantly nucleated village pattern and the west and north in which dispersed habitat is most common. The idealised English village is based on a general 'green village' type (Fig. 6.6). A small closed community facing a central green, often skirted by a road, and containing church, village pump, pond and – the late additions – school and community centre. Often a castle or hall is a reminder of the medieval origins of these villages. This general pattern can be modified considerably in form: street villages are common, the 'green' may be elongated, square or triangular, or have disappeared and given way to a broad central street, and irregular clustered villages – drawn out along roads by modern additions – are all found. The nucleated pattern disappears and gives way to linear settlement under special conditions as in Fen country, where houses are built on higher ground above the marsh. They can hardly be called true villages, yet they are not fully dispersed. The English village varies in size but is always small compared with some continental and Asiatic villages. It did penetrate elsewhere – in the Vale of Glamorgan in Anglo-Norman times, for example – but the nucleated forms in the west often belong to a much later date and are planned. The west is still comparatively free from villages, for we must not confuse them with the rash of service centres which are to be found in the west as elsewhere. The road junction service centre is a comparatively recent addition and has very little to do with the primary occupations of farming.

Generally speaking the English village is a feature which arose between the 5th and 8th centuries, probably reflecting family or kin groups of invading Anglo-Saxons. They were closely tied up with the open-field system of agriculture, and the form is logical in so far as a central point is best for all members of a community whose lands are scattered in strips throughout the open field. Villages must have increased greatly in number between their introduction and the 14th and 15th centuries, for there is evidence of 'daughter' villages being established near the 'parent' foundation and of continual expansion of arable land into the forests covering areas of heavier and poorer soils. Then comes a period when many villages disappeared entirely, leaving sometimes an isolated church, sometimes only the traces of its homesteads, but almost always traces of the plough, best seen in aerial photographs. The causes for the depletion of the rural population in the 14th, 15th and 16th centuries are complex, but the effect on the landscape important, for at this period many open fields were enclosed and the characteristics of the English landscape laid. Arable became pasture, for acres of sheep land could be cared for by one shepherd, and the close strip pattern of the open field gradually gave way to the piecemeal subdivision into fields. The later enclosure acts took the process still farther, though the later enclosures are distinguished by more regular patterns of fields, straight roads and the familiar thorn hedges and ditches. While the landscape was undergoing this radical change there was also a tendency for the villages which disappeared to be replaced by isolated farms, built anew and in the centre of the newly consolidated lands. So the predominantly village pattern is broken by the isolated farm, the concomitant of enclosure (Fig. 6.6). Gone is the exclusively nucleated pattern such as one would find in present-day Hesse, still tied to the open field and the intricate but lonely pattern of strips.

Beyond the lowlands of England, invaders found that in the west and north the systems of tenure and patterns of farming were very different from their own. Today this Celtic 'fringe' is thought of as having a predominantly dispersed settlement, and if one ignores the more obvious additions of the last century or so, this seems to be the case. Again, however, great caution is advisable in generalising to this degree, and even greater caution in dismissing this as a Celtic pattern. The scatter of planned villages in Scotland and plantation Ireland can be easily accounted for: not so easily the many hamlets which relieve the otherwise monotonous scatter. And when we look at the problem historically, confusion increases. The first edition of the Ordnance Survey of Ireland, completed in the 1830's, reveals Ireland as a land of hamlets: in Scotland crofting settlements still have this pattern, but in Wales we have Gerald Cambrensis' word that in 1180 the people inhabited 'neither town nor castle but lived a solitary existence in the woods'. Both in Ireland and Scotland the hamlet – a tiny cluster of six to a dozen houses haphazardly huddling together – is traditionally connected with an open-field system. The single open field, sometimes called the 'in-field', was divided into blocks which were ploughed in rotation. Each block was further subdivided into strips corresponding in numbers to the householders in the settlement. The hamlet – or 'clachan' – was usually on the edge of the arable open field: beyond it was the 'outfield' of pasture: and beyond this again mountain land was held in common to which cattle were sent in summer and where temporary huts might be built. This temporary summer movement (transhumance) is a characteristic of pastoral societies, but perhaps

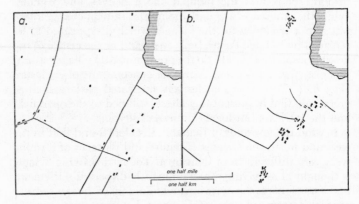

Fig. 6.7. Examination of early O.S. maps of Ireland show that the marked scatter of today (*a*) is the result of the dispersal of the clachans of 1836 (*b*).

too much emphasis has been given to this in the past, giving an impression of an entirely pastoral west which seemed best suited to dispersed habitat. Gradually the role of agriculture is being appreciated in the long development of Celtic rural life, and tied with it is a basically nucleated form. Dispersal in Ireland was late: it followed a great decline in rural population, ravaged by the potato famines of the 1840's. Clachans disintegrated as families disappeared, and land owners sought to sort out the incredible tangle of scattered holdings which had resulted from the system of shared inheritance and subdivision (Fig. 6.7).

Consolidation was common in Ireland from the beginning of the 19th century, and at the end of that century was being controlled by a government commission. With consolidation each new stead was built on its own land. So although one may still find in-fields with their clachans and great numbers of remnants of open fields, the landscape is now one of consolidated fields; and one of the commonest forms is the ladder pattern, where a valley side has been divided into strips: each has its meadow land, arable and mountain pasture, and somewhere near the centre, facing a road traversing the valley side, is the farmhouse. This means that farms are scattered in a line along the road. Dispersed settlement here, then, is secondary – and very recent: indeed the process is still incomplete.

But dispersal in Wales (Fig. 6.8), if it is secondary there, must have been very early. Documentary evidence of the 14th and 15th centuries shows the solitary farmstead – the 'tyddyn' – to be the fundamental unit of settlement. Yet there are hamlet clusters, and some of the earliest evidence suggests that there were such settlements mixed with the scattered habitat. They may well have represented the population which preceded the coming of the Brythonic Welsh: these latter were the free element in the later population, the former were bondmen. The bond vill may have been compact, the free steads were scattered. Even so there is increasing evidence that the first settlements of the free men were clustered near the family arable land. It was only later, when the land was shared among all the children, that land subdivision proceeded so far that new holdings had to be claimed on the former common pasture. Thus inheritance, subdivision and expansion all resulted in dispersal. The links of kinship were maintained, for strong communities can exist in the most scattered settlement, but there was nothing which served as a visible focus – not even the church. Transhumance linked mountain and valley, but expansion meant that hundreds of *hafodtai* (summer houses) became permanent homesteads. Expansion into the common land continued in the early 19th century, when freehold was claimed by building a house in one night. But by this time most 'common land' had disappeared under the enclosure acts, and this phase of

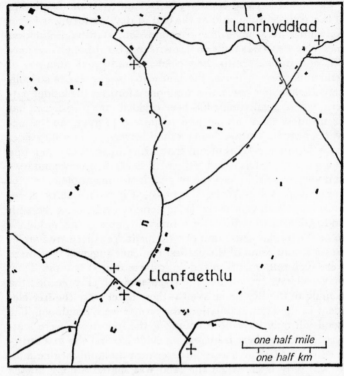

Fig. 6.8. Welsh dispersed settlement (Anglesey). The churches have had no nucleating influence.

expansion is known as 'squatting'. But it added considerably to the scattered habitat.

There is a suggestion in all this that the first pattern is almost invariably nucleated. The hamlet may represent the simplest such unit, much farther back in evolutionary development than the village with its church. To some extent the dispersed settlement of the west of Britain, certainly, can claim to be secondary in the sense that a nucleated form probably preceded it. But the evolution of each part, e.g. Welsh, Irish, Scottish, is very different. That the end result is the same does not mean the process and origin were the same; this is why generalisations are dangerous. There is no simple physical relationship to explain it, but rather a complex of social and economic factors among which we can suggest – (i) land tenure systems; (ii) customs of inheritance; (iii) consolidation; all set against a background of general economy, availability of water, and the degree to which forms are newly introduced or not.

6.4 NEW WORLD SETTLEMENT PATTERNS

So much in the New World is derived from the Old that one would expect a close relationship between rural settlement patterns in America and Europe. But the link is not straightforward: it depends on the period when the new settlements were set up, the kind of society dominant at that time, and the economy, and the last varied enormously with the succession of natural environments through which settlements advanced.

It is not surprising that New England reflects the old in its picturesque villages set among fenced fields and clustering around a church (Fig. 6.9). But the apparent transference was really dependent upon the society which brought it – a number of closely knit communities, whose cultural and religious and political, as well as economic, life centred on the community. Moreover this form was as good an answer as any to the Indian threat.

But neither a tradition of villages nor the Indian threat produced a similar pattern in the early days of the southern colonies. There the colonists were not closed communities which had crossed the Atlantic to preserve their beliefs, but a mixed bag of individualists. Land was held by individuals. It was plentiful and cheap, and the aim was to own land and live on it. Early plantations spread along river sides, for rivers were the highways, and nucleation was absent. And this tied up well with the emerging economy, the cash crops of tobacco, later, rice, and later still, cotton. There were, then, contrasting patterns from earliest colonial times in north and south. There were others like the still predominant Quebec linear pattern, again along a river, each farm extending back in a long narrow

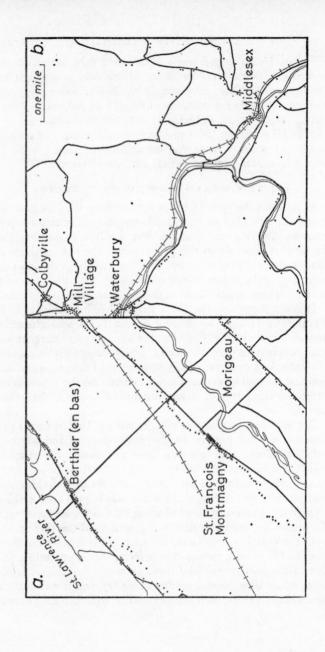

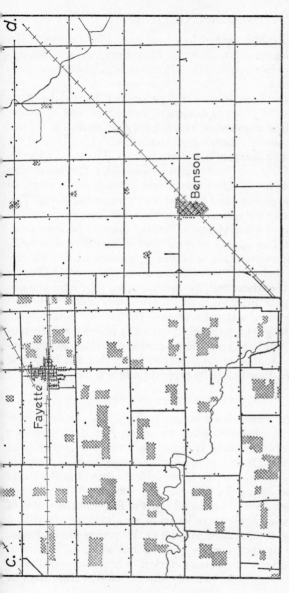

Fig. 6.9. Settlement patterns in North America. The linear villages of Quebec (*a*) reflect the land ownership of the first settlers. New England villages (*b*) are very reminiscent of their English counterparts. Platted land units are characteristic west of the Appalachians, and farms are tied to the roads. In the middle west (*c*) remnants of a forest cover are seen near the centre of each 'square', but in the prairie lands (*d*) the few trees are wind-shelters near the occasional farm.

strip, the houses arranged in a long line. This pattern is also found in the once French lower Mississippi, but it is not uncommon when rivers are the highways, and when frontage is at a premium.

Beyond the Appalachians, and particularly beyond the Ohio, the varieties of patterns disappear. Settlement was no longer haphazard, but controlled by a federal government. Land was accurately surveyed before it was settled, and this produced the familiar grid pattern of the United States. The basic unit was a square of 6 miles, divided into 36 townships. It is interesting that the north wished to perpetuate its nucleated villages in westward expansion and that the south wanted dispersal. Dispersal became the general rule farther west, but the pattern is often broken by the village of market towns: and even community foci like schools have no nucleating effect. The landscape, of immense fields, is broken by solitary farms with tiny clumps of sheltering trees. The market towns are collecting points. In the wheat belt, for instance, they follow the railway line, are quite frequent, and monotonously alike—each with its storage silos, water tower and station and single Main Street. Throughout, the impression is of a planned rural settlement, and until one sees a Hopi pueblo or a Navajo encampment in the south-west, it is easy to forget that this landscape was peopled long before its present pattern arose.

6.5 PLANNED COMMUNITIES

The latter stages of settlement in the U.S.A. are a reminder that not all patterns evolve naturally, but that some are planned before the land is settled, and their distinctive form may be derived from a pure abstract design based on a square or a circle. In Britain this is particularly true of new villages which arose during the 17th and 18th centuries, when the age of reason left its imprint on all parts of life, and the truths of a new scientific age were reflected in the symmetry of a village layout (Fig. 6.10). Estate villages of this period are no longer haphazard or even orderly clusters, but a regular balanced exercise. Perhaps this is more marked in Scotland and Ireland where the village was virtually absent before, rather than in

England, the land of villages. In Wales the planned village is almost non-existent. But in Scotland, the settled period following the '45 rebellion saw the growth of over 150 planned villages. They were not closely related to agriculture. Many were estate villages, some tiny mill villages, some coastal villages; but all absorbed a surplus population which the land could not hold. Their pattern varies from those with a green, resembling some English villages, to some which are very loosely knit, and which by now have all but lost their plan.

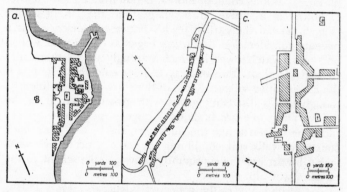

Fig. 6.10. Three examples of planned settlement in Britain. (a) Inveraray, Argyllshire, (b) Milton Abbas, Dorset, and (c) Castlewellan in Co. Down, Northern Ireland.

Planned communities in Ireland, particularly in the north where Scottish and English influence was so great, are more like market towns than villages: but they arose in a country where the market town was non-existent. In a sense all new, i.e. English, settlement was planned, and its main contribution to the landscape, apart from the large country house, was the planned towns of the 17th and 18th centuries. The centre was often a square market place, sometimes out of proportion to the size of the town, or a wide street, nowhere more disproportionate than in Cookstown (Co. Tyrone), where it was based on Dublin's O'Connell Street. (But unfortunately Cookstown never grew beyond its one street!) Sometimes the plan became very elaborate, as in Castlewellan (Co. Down), where one 'square' is an octagon and one a circle, connected by a very broad, tree-lined street (Fig. 6.10(c)). These are impressive in spite of their small size because they are still so foreign to the landscape.

The planned community everywhere indicates new elements, the pushing forward of frontiers, whether in 18th-century Ireland, 19th-century Idaho or 20th-century Hokkaido. It is most striking when it contrasts so markedly with indigenous village patterns. Nothing could be more different from the loose cluster of houses in a native Arab village than the Israeli village (Fig. 6.11). In the earlier Jewish settlements defence was a primary consideration, and many began as desert forts, walled and with a watch tower, in which a strongly united community worked and slept. Two basic types have emerged. The first is the co-operative village. Some of these are arranged linearly, though this is disadvantageous with growth away from the centre: and some are built on a circular pattern, the fields radiating outwards like the sun's rays, the houses, their back courtyard walls still combining to make a protective wall, facing inwards to the community centre, to the school, to the place of worship.

The second type is the collective village or *kibbuz*. This is more directly related to the early fort settlements, because although they are now planned freely, with no conscious defence element, the social organisation is clearly reflected in the functions of the different parts—the living quarters, the common dining and kitchen quarters, the separate farm units, and so on. This is taken to the extreme in the children's *kibbuz*, which is a replica of the larger unit. So plainly may social structure be revealed in settlement form and function.

SUGGESTIONS FOR FURTHER READING

J. O. M. BROEK and J. W. WEBB: *Geography of Mankind* (McGraw-Hill), 1968.

M. D. CHISHOLM: *Rural Settlement and Land Use* (Hutchinson), 1962.

A. DEMANGEON: 'The Origins and Causes of Settlement Types' (in *Wagner and Mikesell*, op. cit.).

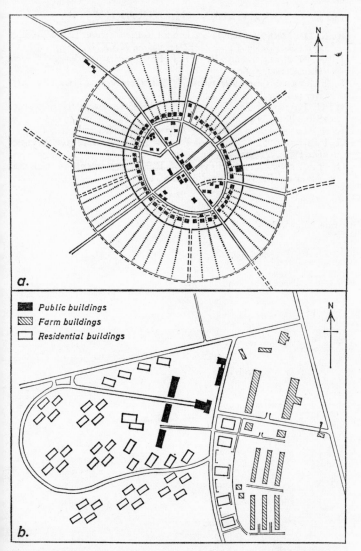

Fig. 6.11. Planned settlements in Israel. The co-operative village (*a*) shows the element of protection and focusing on communal functions: the *kibbuz* (*b*) is completely communal and functions are entirely separated.

Legend:
- Public buildings
- Farm buildings
- Residential buildings

R. E. Dickinson: 'Rural Settlement in the German Lands', *Annals of the Association of American Geographers*, XXXIX, 1949.

J. A. Everson and B. P. Fitzgerald: *Settlement Patterns* (Longman), 1969.

P. Flatres: *Géographie rurale de quatre contrées celtiques* (Plihon), Rennes, 1957.

W. G. Hoskins: *The Making of the English Landscape* (Hodder and Stoughton), 1960.

J. M. Houston: *A Social Geography of Europe* (Duckworth), 1953.

G. Pfeifer: 'The Quality of Peasant Farming in Central Europe' (in *W. L. Thomas*, op. cit.).

G. T. Trewartha: 'Types of Rural Settlement in Colonial America' (in *Wagner and Mikesell*, op. cit.).

Chapter 7

MINING AND MANUFACTURING

7.1 GROWTH OF METAL-WORKING

The discoveries which led societies to become food producers initiated a new and extensive exploitation of the biological world. Equally far-reaching were changes which resulted from the exploitation of mineral resources, of metal-working and the application of power to tools: all of which were eventually to lead to the industrial revolution.

As a toolmaker man has spent all but a fraction of his long existence fashioning stone, first chipping then laboriously polishing the raw material into implements and weapons. Other raw materials were available in the stone age. Exquisite weapons show early men's skill in fashioning bone; and no doubt they were equally skilled in wood, a material which has left few traces. Mineral exploitation in the stone age was small and restricted, though individual examples of flint mines, as at Grime's Caves in East Anglia, are impressive, as are the number of implements which mark prehistoric flint workings: and even at this early stage, certain minerals were carried far from their origin – probably traded – because they were highly valued.

Metal-working came comparatively late, but its arrival marked important epochs in man's history. The prehistoric time scale is traditionally based on technological advances. The old, middle and new stone ages (*palaeolithic, mesolithic* and *neolithic*) give way to bronze age and iron age, and the discoveries and inventions which enabled these metals to be used were radical and had very far-reaching effects. They were Old World inventions, and we must look for the origin of metallurgy in the same general area as for the origin of cereal cultivation. Minerals were not unknown in the New World, for copper, silver and gold were worked in small quantities in Central and

South America; but their limited use required no fundamental discoveries or inventions. Native copper, for example, can be beaten into shapes – utilitarian or ornamental. Copper was used in small quantities in the later stone ages; but it is not a very satisfactory metal for tools and weapons because it is too soft and loses its edge rapidly.

The first radical advance in the Old World was the use of bronze, an alloy of copper and tin. Its production demanded not only the discovery that a small percentage of tin added to copper will produce a more durable metal with a harder edge, not only the knowledge of the location of these resources, but also the invention of a blast furnace which would produce temperatures up to 1,100° C., and the use of charcoal. Copper and tin are often found in quite close proximity in the Near East, but this does not lessen the magnitude of these discoveries. Once the process was mastered and applied also to gold, silver and lead, the casting of implements meant a speedy method of production. The use of metal was extended. Weapons could be multiplied easily, armour could be made, and metal tyres for wheels revolutionise transport.

Iron came later. It may seem surprising that an alloy, bronze, should have preceded iron; but if copper or bronze metallurgy is applied to iron – i.e. if the ore is heated in a simple two chambered oven – although smelting takes place at 600° C. to 700° C., the iron which emerges is almost useless because it is so fouled by slag. It can be hammered out by repeated beating and reheating, but this is a very long and difficult process, and if iron was produced in this way in the 2nd millennium B.C., small wonder that it was a precious metal. The secret of iron smelting was to place the ore directly over the fire with charcoal and to add limestone which fused into the slag and took it away. But such a simple statement sums up momentous discoveries and inventions, which were probably arrived at during the 2nd millennium B.C. by the Hittites of Anatolia. Here there was iron ore and plenty of hardwood too, but these would be meaningless without the inventive genius of the early metallurgists. As long as the process was understood by few only, the metal remained precious, but in the 1st millennium B.C. its use spread greatly in the Near East and into Europe. Iron was a vastly superior metal to bronze, for it could be given a very sharp and durable edge by forging, i.e. rapid cooling, reheating and hammering.

The spread of these ideas, and the spread of implements and weapons, indicate extensive trading throughout Europe and the Near East: this suggests organisation, and also specialisation. A new class of people was emerging which was freed from food-producing, for cereal growing was now ensuring a surplus of food which enabled people to concentrate entirely on these new skills. This is probably the origin of the separateness of the smith, which persists, particularly in simple societies. Among the Badawin, for example, they are a separate caste, shut out from the remainder of society but protected by them because of their skills. And one wonders whether the vagrant tinker is not the last vestige of this in our own society.

The impact of the exploitation of mineral resources was much wider than the growth of metallurgy alone suggests. Men also built houses and monuments: they used stone, clay, sand, as well as timber: and they have gone on quarrying, digging, cutting, destroying in the very act of creating and so modifying their habitat and creating new landscapes.

The scale was modest and the degree of change was necessarily small during the period when men were restricted to the use of tools, i.e. to using their hands alone and the power of their own bodies. Machines, which multiplied man's strength, and which harnessed other kinds of power – animal, wind and water – made further changes more rapid. The wheel was probably the most fundamental invention in this respect, and again it is interesting to note its absence in the New World until introduced from Europe in the 16th century.

The use of simple machines like the wheel and the screw, and of wind and water power, was the basis of man's manufacturing activities until the full flowering of the industrial revolution in Western Europe in the last century. Throughout this long period, which saw the growth and decline of the medieval civilisations and of renaissance Europe, the use of metal was still restricted. Stone and clay were extensively used as building materials, but more than anything else, timber was exploited, until the landscape of parts of Europe changed complexion completely. Timber was not only a fuel: it was one of the most extensively used materials in house construction in Europe. Even the medieval masons could not build their massive Gothic cathedrals without timber scaffolding. Furniture, utensils, vehicles, vessels, waterwheels and windmills were all of timber. Even the smelting of iron resulted in wholesale destruction of forests to supply charcoal. So great was the use of timber in 16th-century Britain, for example, that in Elizabeth's reign laws were passed restricting its use in order to safeguard a supply for making naval vessels.

But although the use of machines was increasing, and although inventions and discoveries were accumulating, manufacturing remained small in scale and geographically dispersed. The larger towns had their numerous workshops, but the location of manufacturing was almost unrestricted. Any stream could turn a millwheel, and few areas could not harness the wind: the unit of power was small—the single mill—and it could be applied almost anywhere in north-west Europe. The result was a scatter of mills and workshops which did little if anything to disturb the rural way of life which predominated.

The series of inventions and discoveries in technology which we call the industrial revolution, and which in Britain was initiated at the end of the 18th century and reached its peak in the second half of the 19th century, brought with it the vast changes in landscape and life which today characterise great areas of north-west Europe, north-eastern U.S.A. and which have now been carried into parts of the other continents. Geographers are concerned with two aspects of this phase, for a new significance was given to two economies, mining and manufacturing, both of which have created their own problems of land use, types of landscape, location factors and settlement. The changes pivot on (a) the vast use of iron as a raw material and (b) the application of steam as a source of power, and consequently the use of coal. Reference was made above to the beginnings of the iron age: it would be much more appropriate to call the 19th century the iron age, when metal began extensively to replace stone and timber as a raw material. The foundation of the new iron technology was laid in the early 18th century when coke smelting replaced charcoal, but the great increase in iron output came at the end of the 18th century and beginning of the 19th century. A revolution in steel-making processes by Bessemer and Siemens meant that steel had virtually replaced iron by the end of the 19th, and its vast production made it a cheap material. The Victorians used iron prodigally. The monuments of their age are made of iron and steel, the vast bridges, railway stations, the Eiffel Tower: miles of rail and giant ocean vessels. On a more humble scale it entered the home in countless ways, from spoon to bedstead.

Coal, the key to iron production, was also the key to power, for it supplied steam, and improved steam engines in the early 19th century were beginning to transform industry. It soon became apparent that the bigger the steam engine the more economical it was, and it was this large unit of power which compelled manufacturers to build mills in which hundreds of people were employed. The fact that the new machines were even more economically run if they were constantly kept going initiated a shift system of workers, which doubled the population dependent on each mill. These last factors meant a vast concentration of people on a restricted number of locations – as near as possible to the supply of coal – and completely changed the pattern of industry and population distribution. Rural life was finally broken, and new relationships were established between society and the habitat, many of which are the bases of the present-day human geography of much of north-west Europe.

The demands of the industrial revolution, particularly in the later phases, when various kinds of steel demanded small quantities of rarer metals, when the spread of electricity demanded copper, when new alloys initiated the exploitation of bauxite, made mining a worldwide economy. Although mining had played its part in the economy of some societies for millennia, it was the vast demand for coal and metal in the last 150 years which was responsible for an activity which has produced its own distinctive landscape.

7.2 DISTRIBUTION AND EFFECTS OF MINING

The world distribution of mining activities is not necessarily that of the distribution of resources, but of the exploitation of some of those resources, reflecting the needs of the societies which are carrying out the exploitation (Fig. 7.1). The distribution reflects three elements:

1. The presence of the minerals themselves. These are widely scattered and are rarely very extensive. They reflect geological factors.

2. The need for the minerals and the incentive to quarry or mine them.

3. The technical ability to abstract the minerals.

The last two are the elements which make the presence of minerals geographically significant. The fact that they are variable elements means that the distribution of mining activity at any one time reflects the culture of that time and of the society which is exploiting the resources. Technical ability and needs change rapidly and this change is reflected in the distribution of mining activities, accentuated by the fact that so many mineral deposits are small and rapidly exhausted.

The map shows, therefore, a very wide distribution. Mining is frequently carried on in areas where men would otherwise be very loath to go: in the northern interior of Canada, in the inhospitable and nearly inaccessible Andean regions, in Chilean and Australian deserts. These places are remote from the relatively fewer areas where minerals are used, and this means that there is constant and widespread movement. This is particularly so today when more emphasis is placed on rarer metals whose supply is often very restricted. For example, all the world's quartz crystals come from Brazil; 89 per cent of the world's molybdenum comes from the United States and only 5 per cent from Chile, the second producer; 80 per cent of the world's nickel comes from Canada and most of the remainder from the U.S.S.R. Modern technology demands an enormous range of minerals, and consequently the transit links are worldwide.

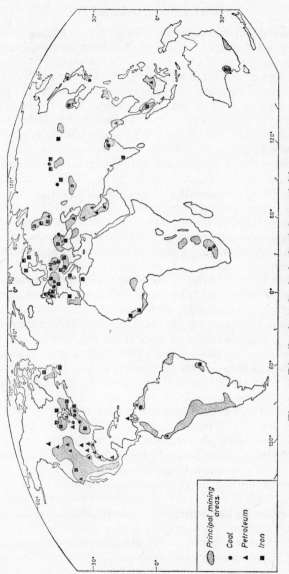

Fig. 7.1. Distribution of principal mining activities.

Three features characterise landscapes which result from mining: (a) the speed with which they arise and the dramatic effects which they can produce, (b) their temporary character –although the effects of mining may be far more permanent– and (c) the difficulties which are overcome in order to exploit mineral resources. Brunhes says of mining: 'The essential characteristic of mineral exploitation is that it fixed man's labours suddenly and for a time being only, at one particular place on the earth's surface.'

Examples of the rapidity of growth of mining communities are found in this country. In the South Wales coalfield the population of the Rhondda Valleys was less than 1,000 in 1851: in 1911 these mining communities numbered 152,000. Even this example does not compare with the suddenness with which mining settlements arise in gold, silver and copper areas. Occupation is here characterised by 'rushes' and towns appear almost overnight. Exploitation of precious minerals in the Rockies time and again gave rise to the almost spontaneous tented community followed quickly by shacks, and in a very small interval a completely platted town. Of such boom towns one of the most spectacular was Dawson, on the Klondyke river. In the spring of 1897, immediately after news of the gold strikes, this tiny frontier post suddenly became a tent camp of 1,500 persons. A year later it was a flourishing town of between 30,000 and 40,000 people with nearly all the amenities of a long-established city. Its hey-day was a brief twelve months. Three years after the appearance of the first tents it was a ghost town of a few hundred people. Kuwait offers a good example of the effects of mining on a simple community. Before the discovery of oil in 1938 this small sheikdom, by virtue of its aridity and intense heat, had a very sparse population of nomadic camel herders. A phenomenal rise in oil production after the Second World War, and the discovery that its proven oil reserves are double those of the United States, have transformed this country. Al Kuwait, formerly nothing more than a market and palace, is now a thriving city of 150,000, and Ahmadi, 30 miles to the south, is an entirely new community of 20,000. This truly exotic development–for even water for these towns must be distilled from the sea—reflects the wealth which is flowing in at the rate of 1 million dollars a day. The two towns have acres of suburban dwellings, and between them possess 55 schools and a college.

The increase of workers and the effect on settlement and landscape is hardly less dramatic in the copper belt of Katanga. Although these mines have been worked since 1900, it was the discovery in 1925 of sulphide ores at depths of 100 feet and more which gave the first real impetus to growth, and in this first boom 30,000 Africans settled near the mines. The number decreased greatly in the 1930's, but during the Second World War it rose again even more dramatically, and in 1954 there were 424,000 persons on the field, the town of Kitare having a population of 80,000, including 10,000 Europeans.

No one foresees the immediate extinction of Kuwait and Katanga: the oil reserves of the former are immense, and Katanga is thought to have 20 million tons of copper in its ores. Yet extinction, partial or complete, is the ultimate fate of mining settlements. In a complex industrialised region such as South Wales the effect is masked, partly by the fact that coal mining is still carried on, and partly by the introduction of other industries. But even so, decline in coal production brings decline in population.

Where mining is the only activity the exhaustion of a lode of precious metal leads to immediate withdrawal; and the history of Dawson shows that this can be as dramatic as the original growth of settlement. Ghost towns are a feature of the mining areas of the Rocky Mountains, empty towns which, in their very brief life, boasted prosperous main streets, hotels and even, in one case, an opera house. The fleeting nature of settlement is particularly true around gold and silver mines where the lode may be small. If the lode is considerable, then even a purely mining town will have a longer life, as at Butte, Montana, which is dependent on one vast copper lode. The disappearance of so many mining communities underlines the fact that exploitation takes place in areas where, very often, no other kind of economy can be practised, or where the alternative economy is one which supports only a very sparse population.

One of the most dramatic features of mining is the way in which men will overcome almost insuperable difficulties in order to exploit mineral wealth. Logical links with the habitat seem to be broken, and nonsense made of the simple relationships between habitat and society which geographers often stress.

To obtain mineral wealth men will defy the most inhospitable conditions. Kuwait is one example of this. The development of the Chuquicamata copper deposits in northern Chile is another. This mine is in the Atacama desert, where the rainfall averages 25 mm/1 in per year; nevertheless, here is found a community of 25,000 people who are dependent on water brought from the Andes, on food brought in entirely by truck and rail, and on power (electricity) brought from the coast, 145 km away. This is the biggest single copper mine in the world, and over 300,000 tons are produced annually. The great nitrate deposits of Chile are worked under equally difficult conditions, all foods and power having to be brought in from outside.

The mining of copper in the middle Andean area of Chile illustrates even more dramatically man's determination to exploit mineral wealth. In these mountain regions mining takes place at 3,650 m/12,000 ft, physiologically a difficult altitude for men to work. Drifts are cut into the mountain side at the bottom of canyons, and shafts worked upward for 600 m/ 2,000 ft: the ore is collected by gravity. Here there is literally no site in the usual sense for settlement, and the miner's quarters are excavated into the mountain side, being accessible from the shaft only. A small spur a mile downstream is the site of a town, mill and waste deposits; but the smelters, on the first reasonable site, are 13 km away.

Even more desolate are the tin mines of Bolivia, worked at 4,570 m/15,000 ft, near the limit of permanent snow, where all materials and food must be brought in from elsewhere.

These are extreme illustrations of mineral exploitation in difficult and empty areas, but they could be multiplied, for technologically man is now equipped to tap oil in the Sahara or from the floor of the Caribbean, and it seems that no conditions are too difficult for him to overcome temporarily, at least, in his quest for minerals.

However brief the exploitation and however temporary the settlement, mining leaves its permanent marks and distinctive landscape. These are not merely the scars of a quarry or the mouth of a drift, but the vast quantities of waste which are a by-product of mining. It leaves a landscape of waste. Of the

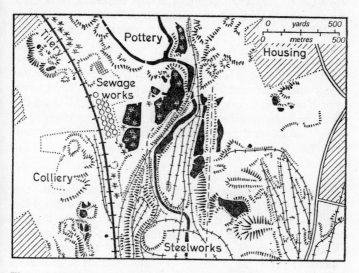

Fig. 7.2. The landscape of waste which is associated with mining and heavy manufacturing (the Potteries).

17,000 tons of copper ore mined daily in northern Chile, 16,000 tons are waste. The tin content of Bolivian ores is 2·1 per cent; 96 per cent is eliminated as waste. The complement of the shafthead is the dump: and even where, as in deep mining, the shafts and galleries are hidden, the dumps and tips of spoil heaps are very apparent. North Cardiganshire has its lead spoil heaps, Snowdonia its slate tips, South Wales its slag heaps and its enormous coal tips, Cornwall has its white kaolin tips. Lead waste stubbornly rejects plant growths and slate is also defiant;

but in Britain slag heaps and coal tips have over many years become grassed over. They have become part of the landscape, difficult to dissociate from the mountain side: indeed plant colonisation on some has now extended to tree growth, and the former blight becomes an amenity. Only fairly recently has the problem of waste been assessed and societies become conscious of this landscape. The Victorians were prodigal: the word conservation belongs to this century. Much waste can be utilised, some can be returned to the galleries and shafts. In open-cast mining, which temporarily causes the greatest seeming devastation, soil which has been ripped away is replaced when the coal has been removed and the former land use restored. Waste dumps are not the only signs of mining. Underground working causes subsidence and the sagging of the surface. Water gathers in such hollows, forming the distinctive flashes of Midland districts. Subsidence affects roads and houses, and everywhere overgrown mineral lines and derelict gear mar the landscape (Fig. 7.2).

7.3 MANUFACTURING–MAIN TYPES

Much more significant than mining in non-agricultural economies is manufacturing. It is difficult to make sharp distinctions between stages in the process from, say, a mineral resource like iron ore and a finished product such as a complicated steel machine, though it is clear in this case that the process of producing the steel is quite separate from that of making the machine. But the word manufacturing will be used here to cover the whole range of processes which transform raw materials into commodities, whether the commodities are used directly or are themselves used as material for further processing.

As the word implies, until very recently in man's history manufacture was the product of handcraft, and this is still so over large areas of the world's surface. The weaver, the potter and craftsmen in wood and metal supply the needs of simple societies: although essential they play a minor role in what are overwhelmingly agricultural communities. Their activities produce no great changes in either forms of settlement or structure of society. Many crafts are ancillary to home life: even the more specialised demand no more than small workshops or kilns. It is possible for such crafts to become highly commercialised, without altering their basic structure, as they did, for example, in post-medieval Europe. But the radical changes came only with the industrial revolution. Largely because of the demands of steam power, the small work unit based on a workshop was ousted and was replaced by the factory or mill system. Moreover the machine introduced the concept of mass production and the concentration of output at restricted centres. The familiar paraphernalia of manufacturing industries now became fixed, the massive factories and chimneys, and the great and increasing concentrations of people which were needed to satisfy industrial demands. Concentration was the keynote.

One of the basic activities in manufacturing is the production of *iron and steel*, themselves so essential for further processing. Reference has already been made to the early stages of the growth of metallurgy: today iron and steel are the overwhelmingly important metals throughout the world. A series of technical innovations put Britain in a dominating position in 19th-century production, first in iron then in steel. In 1820 Britain produced a quarter of the world output of 1·7 million tons of iron; in 1840, just under a half of the world's 3·3 million tons; and in 1860, one-half the world output of 7·4 million tons. From 1870 onwards steel began to take the place of iron and became dominant in the 20th century. The two great regions of steel production are north-west Europe and the U.S.A., this location depending largely on the availability of raw materials, good transport, and a market for steel.

Britain itself has several steel centres, the north-east, South Wales, the Clyde area and the Midlands. When initiated, steel production was found largely in the same location as the iron mills which had depended much on the close association of good coking coal, limestone, and local deposits of iron ore; but the last diminished rapidly, and it was easy accessibility of ports which underlay the continued production of steel in most of these regions. High-quality ores are imported from Sweden, Spain and North Africa. In more detail this change from local to imported ores in South Wales also meant a migration of the industry from the northern rim of the coalfield (Merthyr, Dowlais, Aberdare) to the ports (Cardiff, Swansea and Port Talbot); it was government interest and policy which resuscitated Ebbw Vale. Another European area blessed with excellent coking coal, easy transport and good ores is split by international boundaries. Ores are concentrated in Lorraine, coal in the Ruhr; but this entire region, north-east France, the Ruhr, Belgium and Luxembourg, is now combined in a European steel community. To the north, steel production in east central Sweden is largely dependent on the local ores. Farther east the Silesian steel centres link the west European areas with the Russian. The earliest centres in Russia were based on the coal deposits of the Ukraine, with subsidiary centres near Moscow and Leningrad. But in the last twenty years great developments have been taking place even farther east. The Ural iron deposits have been linked not only with the coal deposits of Karaganda, but with the Kuznetsk basin: ore is taken back to Kuznetsk and this basin is now a major steel centre.

The steel belt of the United States embraces the north-east manufacturing area and extends westward to Gary and Chicago. The two great bases are the good coking coals of Pittsburgh and the Lake Superior ores. One hardly needs to be reminded that this is also the region of consumption, where so many other manufacturing industries are based on steel. The Great Lakes portion of this belt extends from Duluth to Buffalo, but it is concentrated on Chicago and Cleveland. Pittsburgh has long been a centre in the eastern district, but comparatively recently there have been several significant changes of emphasis and some innovations. Although the raw materials in the vicinity are rather low grade, Birmingham, Alabama, has developed on local ore, coal and flux. Sparrow's Point, Maryland, on the other hand, depends on sea transport for iron ore, most of which comes from Labrador and Venezuela; its great advantage is its nearness to consuming areas. Trenton, New Jersey, has similar advantages and is beginning to develop on Venezuelan ore. A fairly recent departure from the more traditional pattern is the development of steel production in

Utah, for although there are adequate raw materials fairly near, this area depends partly on federal government sponsoring to offset the disadvantages of distant markets.

One of the world's leading manufactures is *textiles*. It has some claim to prior consideration, not only because of its very long history as a handcraft, but because so many of the early steps in industrialisation and the use of machines were introduced in textile manufacture at the very beginning of the industrial revolution. These took place in 18th-century England, where woollen goods already had a long history while cotton cloth was still an exotic article imported from India. Between 1733 and 1785 major advances like the waterframe, powerloom, flyshuttle and spinning jenny, transformed textile manufacturing; the industry soon saturated the home market with cotton goods and began the overseas expansion which so transformed the north of England. In the 19th century England was the world's workshop in textiles. In 1950 the United States was by far the greatest producer of cotton fabrics, though the U.S.S.R. and India were also very important, followed by the United Kingdom, France and Germany: the last three were also major producers of cotton yarn. The United States led in wool production, both yarn and fabric, closely followed by the United Kingdom, France and Germany. The United States was also far ahead of the United Kingdom, Germany and Japan in rayon production. Apart from these leading countries there has been much less concentration of textile manufacturing in the last two decades, and the so-called underdeveloped countries are increasingly sharing in production. There is a tendency, however, for rayon and nylon production to be concentrated still in the older established industrial centres.

The introduction of machinery, the crux of the industrial revolution, initiated another great branch of manufacturing—that of *machine tools*. The need is implicit in what has been said about the mechanisation of textile manufacturing, but the need elsewhere is no less arresting. Agriculture, for example, has been transformed by the introduction of machinery and later by the substitution of the horse by the tractor. Transport is a dominant need, and the manufacturing of all kinds of tools and machines. It is not surprising that a third of the manufacturing industries in the world produce machine tools. In the 19th century Britain again dominated world output, but the United States has increased its production of machine tools so much that this industry now accounts for more than half the total in that country. The dominance of one or a few countries has now decreased very considerably. Whereas in 1890 the United Kingdom launched 80 per cent of the world's shipping output, this had already fallen to a third before the Second World War, during which the United States became a major producer. Sweden has always been high on the list of ship-building countries. The United Kingdom also dominated railway and rolling stock production during the last century, but all countries now share in this. Most manufacturing countries also share greatly in the production of cars, though the United States is dominant in this growing industry. In 1965 the United States produced 7·7 million cars. West Germany was in second place with 2·6 million and the United Kingdom third with 1·8 million. Manufacture of aircraft is newer, and rather more restricted to comparatively wealthy countries with a long tradition of manufacturing. The United States and the United Kingdom are important producers; so are France, Germany and the U.S.S.R.

Food processing is one of the few manufacturing industries which are important outside the well-established industrial countries, for it is based on an agricultural surplus. It is true that all states share in this industry, although its mechanisation was late. It was a concomitant of the great surge of urbanisation of the 19th century, the divorce, for so many people, from fresh and immediate supplies of food: and it has increased enormously with the improvement in standard of living which has typified Western countries in this century. We are concerned not so much with the food processing that is carried on in the home, but that which serves towns and cities everywhere: milling, baking, dairy manufacturing, canning and freezing. Because of the modern demand, a large percentage of employed people are found in these manufacturing industries in most countries–e.g. 10·9 per cent in the United States: but naturally its importance increases very greatly in those count-tries with an agricultural surplus, like Australia (13·8 per cent), New Zealand (18·6 per cent) and Venezuela (61·4 per cent).

When meat production began to be concentrated in the world's great temperate grasslands, the distance from the market was a considerable problem. In the 19th century meat processing in the United States was concentrated at the mid-century railheads, the junction of the producing and consuming areas. Packing and processing became important, therefore, in Chicago, Kansas City, Omaha, St. Paul and St. Louis. Speed was still essential in transporting meat, and the problem was not resolved until the introduction of refrigeration. Then the seaports of Argentina became processing centres, and Australia and New Zealand could fill the demands of north-west Europe. In Europe meat processing is much less concentrated. Canning is very dispersed, but, like refrigeration, it has opened a new field in manufacturing since the 1880's.

The last of the important manufacturing industries is the *chemical* industry. This is the latest, and follows what some would call a 'chemical revolution' at the end of the 19th century. Its products are amazingly varied, from synthetic fibres, explosives, drugs and medicines and paints, to soap and heavy chemicals. This great range in products parallels a range in production methods and in raw material. Indeed it is not necessarily dependent on any raw material because it can chemically change the very structure of material. This means that abundant and cheap material is used. Unless this material is very bulky, it also means that the manufacturing is located near the areas of consumption. Chemical industries are found in most large cities; in the United States, for example, New York, Philadelphia, Pittsburg and Chicago are all important centres.

7.4 DISTRIBUTION AND LOCATION OF MANUFACTURING

The characteristics of the distribution of industrial activity are these (Fig. 7.3):

(a) The overwhelming concentration in north-west Europe and north-east America.

L

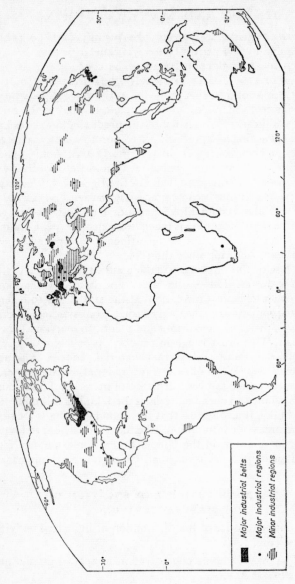

Fig. 7·3. Distribution of principal manufacturing regions.

Major industrial belts
Major industrial regions
Minor industrial regions

(b) The less concentrated but still conspicuous manufacturing areas of the U.S.S.R.

(c) The relatively little and scattered industrial activity in the underdeveloped countries of the world.

(d) The close relationship between manufacturing and cities in newer countries.

This broad pattern can be equated with the stage of development of each country, and with the historical fact that modern industry originated in Great Britain, France and Germany and spread to the New World, where a similarity in culture and level of living meant its immediate adoption and development. Its spread elsewhere has been slower and more restricted, partly because demands and needs are very different at other cultural levels.

In more detail the location of industry within this world pattern is the result of the interplay of very many factors, and it is one of the tasks of the economic geographer, in explaining location, to weigh these factors carefully. If the raw materials of the industry in question are bulky, costly to transport, or are perishable, manufacturing may well be undertaken as near the raw materials as possible. If the manufactured product is perishable then the location will usually be very near the market. On the other hand the type of energy used in manufacturing may be vital. It is a disadvantage for an industry using coal to be very distant from its coal supply. Oil is relatively mobile because its transport by sea is easy: industries do not grow up in the Middle East, but at the European terminals of oil routes. Electricity is very mobile and can now be transported up to 600 miles. It is also very adaptable: the same supply will light a tiny bulb or move a vast engine. This, plus its easy transmission, means that the former concentration which characterised coal-using industries may well be broken down under certain circumstances and units dramatically reduced. It enables industries to become scattered again if this is desirable. Dependence on coal and lignite has decreased greatly in recent years. In 1929 70 per cent of world energy came from coal; in 1958, only 50 per cent came from coal, whereas oil had increased from 14 per cent to 28 per cent in the same period and hydro-electricity from 5 per cent to 9 per cent. Countries with little or no coal can now increase manufacturing. Norway depends on hydro-electricity for 77 per cent of the total energy it uses and very little on coal (5 per cent): Denmark depends increasingly on oil (54 per cent). The United Kingdom still derives 81 per cent of its energy from coal. New sources of energy, then, are changing location patterns, both on a world scale – enabling countries formerly with no coal to become manufacturing centres – and in details of location within manufacturing countries.

But in addition to raw materials, markets, transport and sources of energy, detailed location depends on costs of production, particularly where labour costs are very high in relation to the cost of the manufactured articles, on labour itself, on pools of special skills, and on the availability of capital which, although it may move easily within countries, rarely moves as freely across state frontiers.

There are other factors which the geographer, in his preoccupation with raw materials perhaps, is apt to forget. Some industries work more economically in association with others: steel users are attracted to steel centres, and small industries with common needs often cluster in cities, giving distinctive quarters like the clothing and furniture-making districts of London. Inertia can also be powerful – i.e. the continuation of an industrial activity after the factors which determined its locations have ceased to be important. Lastly one should not forget increasing government activity which often overrides purely economic factors. On a large scale examples are found in Russia's development of the trans-Ural industrial region, of Kuznetz and Baikal; in the establishing of steel plants in Utah and of the Tennessee Valley Authority. On a smaller scale, the development areas of the United Kingdom, or the establishing of new industries in Northern Ireland by giving loans and grants, are examples of political factors affecting the distribution of manufacturing industries.

SUGGESTIONS FOR FURTHER READING

G. Alexanderson: *Geography of Manufacturing* (Prentice Hall), 1967.

R. C. Estall and R. O. Buchanan: *Industrial Activity and Economic Geography* (Hutchinson), 1961.

N. S. Ginsburg: *Atlas of Economic Development* (Chicago), 1961.

G. Manners: *The Geography of Energy* (Benn), 1964.

N. J. Pounds: *The Geography of Iron and Steel* (Hutchinson), 1959.

W. S. Thatcher: *Economic Geography* (English Universities Press), 1961.

R. S. Thoman: *The Geography of Economic Activity* (McGraw-Hill), New York, 1962.

K. L. Wallwork: 'Land Use Problems and the Evolution of Industrial Landscapes', *Geography*, XLV (4), 1960.

W. S. and E. S. Woytinsky: *World Population and Production* (Twentieth Century Fund), 1968.

Chapter 8

TOWNS AND CITIES (1)

Before discussing towns and cities it is necessary to define them and to suggest how many of the world's people live in towns. The first task offers almost insurmountable difficulties because of the number of definitions of an urban settlement. Implicit in all definitions is the accepted fact that an urban population is a permanent sedentary group of people who are not mainly concerned in primary food production. But most countries have different criteria, of function, government or even size. The extreme functional definition is the simple Israeli one that a town is a non-agricultural settlement, presumably of any size; the most vague is that of Chile, where a town is a centre with urban characteristics; the simplest are those which merely go by size, as in Canada, where all settlements over 1,000 are called urban. Presumably countries equate change of function with size, but this differs widely in various parts of the world; for Colombia the dividing line between rural and urban is 1,500, in Argentina the definition of a town is a settlement over 2,000, and in the United States over 2,500. In Asiatic countries villages may be so large that an even greater figure has to be qualified, as in India, where a town is a settlement of over 5,000 which also has urban characteristics. In the United Kingdom a vast range in size is possible within the definition of a town as a settlement which comes within the local government classification of borough or urban district. Form of government also decides what is a town in South Africa; but in Rhodesia the word town is confined to European settlements—its urban population lives in the 'nine main European towns and neighbouring mines, locations and compounds'.

Any discussion concerning the degree of urbanisation of the

world's population must therefore be made with this in mind. Generally speaking a numerical index must be chosen which excludes large rural settlements, although this eliminates many small settlements with purely urban functions in Europe and parts of European-settled countries.

By almost any criterion it is a minority only of the world's peoples who live in towns and cities, as the following table shows:

Size of urban settlement	Number	Population in millions	Percentage of world population
Over 5,000 people	27,600	717	30
,, 20,000 ,,	5,500	507	21
,, 100,000 ,,	875	314	13
,, 500,000 ,,	133	158	7
,, 1 million ,,	49	101	4

This means that nearly three-quarters of the world's people are still at the peasant/agricultural stage, and that this is a rural world in spite of the fact that urbanisation is more advanced than it has ever been. Furthermore, the regions where urbanisation is very advanced are few, although some degree of urbanisation has spread everywhere. This is shown in the following table:

	Percentage living in cities of over:	
	20,000	100,000
World	21	13
Oceania	47	41
N. America	42	29
Europe	35	21
U.S.S.R.	31	18
S. America	26	18
C. America	21	12
Asia	13	8
Africa	9	5

This table can be discussed better in the light of another, show ing the most urbanised countries (in or about 1950).

	Percentage living in cities of over 20,000	Rank of percentage in towns over 100,000
U.K.	66·8	4
Australia	56·7	1
Holland	56·4	8
Hawaii	55·5	2
New Zealand	49·3	6
Argentina	48·2	5
Israel	45·7	3
United States	42·8	11
Belgium	42·2	7
Germany	41·7	12
Japan	41·7	13
Chile	40·0	15
Denmark	37·7	14
Austria	36·7	10
Uruguay	36·2	8

The first interesting thing is that in the second table there are few European countries in this list in spite of one's precon-ceptions that Europe is a continent of towns and cities: and in spite of the fact that the cities of the newer countries are all derived from Europe. The second is the exclusiveness of the European tradition, for Japan is the only country whose cities are not European derived. The other Asiatic exception is Israel, a new country which is almost purely a transplantation of the urban civilisation of Europe on the mainland of Asia. The third outstanding feature is the high degree of urbanisation in the 'new' countries like Australia and New Zealand and, more surprisingly, Argentina, Uruguay and Chile.

Many of these facts are explicable in terms of the relation-ship between urban and rural in these countries. In European countries, despite the long tradition of urbanisation, there is still a balance of rural population. This is least marked in Eng-land and Wales, where the percentage of urban population is extremely high (80·7 per cent), but it is still a considerable element in Spain, where only 37·0 per cent of the population is urban, and overwhelmingly important in East European countries like Yugoslavia, where only 16·2 per cent is urban, a figure comparable with India (18·0 per cent) or Morocco (18·5 per cent). Many new countries were settled by Europeans after urbanisation had reached a high peak in Europe, and these are, moreover, countries in which extensive agriculture has replaced intensive agriculture, and the manpower employed in food growing is comparatively small. Consequently Australia, despite its primary production capacity, is 68·9 per cent urban and Canada is 69·6 per cent. The United States is 69·9 per cent urban. South Africa, with a high indigenous population, has a lower proportion, 42·6 per cent. In South America, Argentina and Chile have very high proportions (62·5 per cent and 67·2 per cent respectively), but the average for South America is reduced by other states (Colombia 36·3 per cent, Brazil 45·1 per cent, Paraguay 34·6 per cent and Ecuador 28·5 per cent) in which a high rural population, often indigenous, predominates. Existing peasant/farming communities are the main factor which explain low urbanisation. Where Western urban life has arrived late and suddenly then the percentage may be very high, as in Israel (83·9 per cent), or Bahrein (63·0 per cent); in the latter, in former arid nomad territory, there are now two large urban settlements which are in all ways alien to the country. In the old countries of north-west Europe then, urban life has increased gradually; in new agricultural lands, it appeared 'ready made' and increased rapidly; in some, like Bahrein, it appeared almost spontaneously.

8.2 ORIGIN AND GROWTH OF URBANISATION

Urbanisation is a process which can be traced back historically to its origins in the prehistoric civilisations of the Old and New Worlds. An outline of this development may be helpful in understanding the underlying reasons for towns and cities, their function and their relationship with rural communities.

The greatest necessary condition for urban life is to be found in the so-called neolithic revolution – i.e. the change from food gathering and hunting to food producing – which preceded it.

The word revolution is misleading in one sense, for the change was not a very sudden one. In Egypt it is not easy to pinpoint clearly which culture in a long sequence can properly be thought of as the first settled agricultural community, for gathering and hunting persisted with agriculture for a long time. But the word revolution does indicate the magnitude of the change. As already pointed out in Chapter 5, sometime between 9000 B.C. and 5000 B.C., in the Middle East, inventions and discoveries culminating in the domestication of animals and the cultivation of plants enabled men to change their economy, to produce food and to live in permanent settlements. Evidence shows such a development in Egypt, Mesopotamia and in peasant communities west of the Indus Valley; and in a wide region linking these early centres, suggesting a continuum of neolithic conditions. Under similar riverine conditions, the same thing happened in China, but later in time; and later still in the New World maize planting became the basic economy in Central America. In all these cases peasant communities eventually gave rise to urban communities.

One basic reason for this was the ability of these peasant communities to grow more food than a gathering economy could provide, and so allow for a growing population as well as freeing men from the hand to mouth existence which characterised the simpler economies. The rhythm of the agricultural cycle, tied to seasonal growth and to river regimes in the Old World civilisations, gave man leisure. For the first time he had not only a surplus of food, but surplus time and energy, all prerequisites of the diversification of society and division of labour which now took place. For some members of the society could, in this way, be freed from food producing entirely, and the first severance from the soil was made. Moreover the art of irrigation is one which needs organisation; the communities which gave rise to the first towns were not haphazard groups of people, but fairly closely knit societies.

In these communities, discoveries and inventions were already growing, but for the development of material culture were sadly lacking in some things. The Nile had neither timber nor copper, Sumeria had little timber and neither stone nor ores, and the Indus valley lacked many raw materials. This could be overcome only by exchange and trade. Already at the beginning of civilisation there is abundant evidence of trade in the Middle East, and as raw materials were brought in, so they were manufactured by specialists. Former, small, self-sufficing peasant communities now became economically interdependent.

By 3000 B.C. there were true urban societies in the Middle East in which some people were manufacturers, some merchants and traders, some officials and some priests. Into the hands of the last group fell much of the organisation of society. Possibly, through the keeping of temple accounts and observing seasonal cycles, the priestly caste initiated enormous advances in abstract thought, and contributed to the complex arithmetic and astronomy of these early civilisations.

In the above brief outline are all the essentials of urban life: the agricultural surplus which allows the urban population to divorce itself from food production; the town as a focus of a producing region, and as a centre for exchange of goods from outside the region; the rise of artisans and manufacturers; the division of labour and the division of society into classes each with its special task; and all this a reflection of complex organisation which makes the town a single unit, though closely connected with its region.

These prehistoric cities were also usually clearly distinguished from the old peasant villages by monumental architecture, another indication of surplus labour and surplus time: the temples and pyramids of Egypt, the ziggurats and tombs of Sumeria, the pyramids of Yucatan. So rose Memphis and Thebes, Babylon and Nineveh, Harappa and Mohenjodaro, Tikal and Chichinitza (Fig. 8.1).

Some idea of the complexity of urban life in a city of 2000 B.C. may be gathered from a brief description of Harappa in the Indus valley. This walled city, which covered an area of about 2·6 sq km, was divided into a regular grid, making twelve blocks by the intersection of two east–west and three north–south streets, each about 9 m wide. Inside most blocks was a maze of smaller streets bounded by brick walls, for the houses

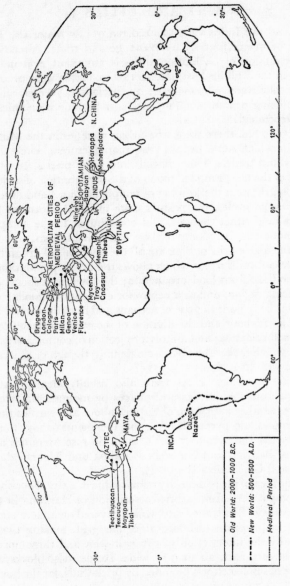

Fig. 8.1. The pre-industrial urban civilisations.

METROPOLITAN CITIES OF
MEDIEVAL PERIOD

Bruges
London
Cologne
Paris
Milan
Genoa
Venice
Florence

N.CHINA

Harappa
INDUS Mohenjodaro

Nineveh MESOPOTAMIAN
Babylon
Ur

Mycenae
Troy
Cnossus
Luxor
Memphis
Thebes   EGYPTIAN

AZTEC
MAYA

Teotihuacan
Texcuco
Mayapan
Tikal

INCA

Cuzco
Nazed

Old World: 2000–1000 B.C.
New World: 500–1500 A.D.
Medieval Period

faced inwards to courtyards, and the only access was a door. Some houses had bathrooms and rubbish chutes, and the town had a drainage system. In one quarter were groups of identical small houses – probably workers' quarters, reminiscent of similar houses in our own industrial cities – and nearby a huge granary. It is difficult to particularise on the monumental architecture, for there is nothing in the excavated ruins corresponding to pyramid or temple; but one block forms a raised platform, the 'citadel', whose most easily distinguishable feature is an immense tank or bath, but which has around it a complex of buildings which suggest it might have been the centre of religion and administration (the tank is still an important religious focus in India). Harappa is a peak of achievement in early town planning, one of the forerunners of the cities of today.

The cities of the Indus, Mesopotamia and the Nile valley disappeared. Many of the monuments remained, for the pyramids were built for eternity. The civilisations waned and were overcome. Harrapa became a mound of mud bricks on top of which a new peasantry built a village. But the idea of the town was not lost. It was transmitted elsewhere. Even while the early civilisations flourished the idea spread to all those regions where trade was maintained. As Sumeria declined, Syria and Asia Minor took over. On Crete there rose the city of Knossos, and from there and Asia Minor the tools and ideas of civilisation spread to Greece. Here the idea of the city flourished anew. It would be a mistake to imagine these as huge cities, for the Greek concept of the city state included the rural area around the city on which its very life depended, and the population of the whole state might be as little as 70,000, of which perhaps a quarter were city dwellers. It is true that some outgrew their rural base: manufacturing and trade enabled the urban population to increase in proportion, and again this implied spreading and colonising until the whole of the Mediterranean shared the influences of urban life. And so the ideas of town life passed to Rome and spread throughout much of Western Europe. Rome itself, another peak of achievement in urban life, soon outstripped its local food supply. It was an imperial centre: its greatest subsidiary was Alexandria, which funnelled the corn supply of the Nile to the Roman Empire, but which was also in its own right a centre of administration, learning and culture. Roman cities also dominated trade routes, and the Romans had trading and military centres throughout Western Europe. The town was an instrument of Roman civilisation.

One example of a Roman town will suffice. Verulamium, the St. Albans of today, covered a site of about 80 ha/ 200 acres and was oval (unlike the usual rectangular plan): it had a large defensive ditch and a wall with four gates and a series of towers. In the centre was the market hall and a monumental forum, and nearby a theatre (which has been excavated and can still be seen). The residential quarter had fairly large houses based on the court plan, well spread out and with no congestion – very different from the shopping centre, which was crowded with buildings. Most Roman towns in Britain were rather smaller – about 100 acres would be an average site – but all had their market place, administration centre and temples, and the different social classes were clearly differentiated in the several quarters of the town. Such towns would be not unlike the smaller market towns of today.

In their turn the towns and cities of imperial Rome declined. Their story ends in the Dark Ages. Civilisation retracted, organisation disintegrated, and Europe generally relapsed into small more self-sufficient units. Peasant communities re-established themselves. Those cities which did not disappear were the shells of cities, the trappings of urbanism without its life. The city was to emerge in new guise in medieval Europe.

But while urban life was flickering in Europe it was growing steadily in the New World to reach a zenith about a thousand years ago. Excavations in Yucatan and Guatemala suggest that these cities reached an immense size, but we should be careful not to read into them the pattern of urban life which had distinguished Old World cities. The Mayan city was more dispersed; it graded imperceptibly into agricultural land, so that the calculations of immense populations must include many who were not townsfolk in the sense implied so far. But in the centre the Mayan city was distinguished by its wonderful stepped pyramids, temples, courts and plazas – all loosely grouped together. Around these were the dwellings of society's leaders, priests, astronomers and nobility, the social grades gradually declining away from the centre.

In Europe towns and cities re-emerged in medieval times. In the awakening and stirring of European peoples from the 11th century onwards, two elements were probably very important: the increase in trading, and the need for defence. The market, central in town life and symbolising the link between the town region and the town, came to life, and with increasing political stability markets extended their scope. Much of Western Europe was becoming linked by trade, and the itinerant merchant certainly played a part in this revival. As market and town became divorced from the castle so townsfolk knit themselves into a close community and protected themselves with walls and ditches. Behind this emergence of towns was the fact that agriculture was steadily improving, forests were being cleared and land reclaimed. Food was increasing and so was the population. There was a sudden surge in urban growth. Paris at the end of the 12th century had 100,000 people and at the end of the 13th 240,000. Florence in 1280 had 45,000 people; in 1339, 90,000. These were among the great cities. Some, like Paris, were centres of exceptionally rich regions, others were entrepots. London, Bruges, Cologne, Genoa, Milan and Venice complete the list of medieval metropolitan cities, for there were few towns over 50,000 (Fig. 8.1). Most urban centres were local market towns, centred on market place and church, the latter almost always a monumental achievement and a symbol of community, cohesion and wealth. The guilds of craftsmen belong to this period, too, as do the oldest universities (Bologna 1100, Paris 1150, Oxford 1170.)

The next phase is not so much an increase in towns generally as an enormous increase of a few particular cities at the expense of others – the capital cities of the great states which were gradually emerging from the consolidation and amalgamation of piecemeal territories. The capital city, a renaissance phenomenon, reflected the concentration of the surplus and wealth of a state; here was the centre of government and here the head of state lived. Surplus energy and wealth went into monumental palaces; and all the specialised strata of society flocked to the King's court. In 1400 London had a population of 50,000; at the end of the 17th century it was 700,000, whereas Bristol and Norwich were still about 30,000, and York and Exeter were the only other two English towns which could muster more than 10,000.

But the greatest phase of urban growth was still to come, and was a response to another event which merits the term revolution. This was the accumulation of technical advances based on coal and iron which we call the industrial revolution. We should be careful in assigning definite dates to this period, because the innovations accumulated slowly and at different times in different countries, but in Britain it is usually assumed that it became a vital factor in the life of the country in the late 18th century, and that it reached a peak in the second half of the 19th century. Here was something which affected, not a few centres as in medieval times, or capital cities as in renaissance times, but areas wherever mineral deposits warranted the rise of industry, and urbanisation, rather than urban growth, now reached an unprecedented level. This was the stage at which people turned from the country to the town, for urbanisation was accompanied by rural depopulation. It also inaugurated the era of the super city. In 1800 there was not one city in Europe with a million people, though London had a population of over 950,000 and Paris over 500,000. By 1850 Paris had passed the one million and London the two million mark. By 1900 nine other cities had joined the 'million' group: Berlin, Vienna, Moscow and St. Petersburg, New York, Chicago, Philadelphia and Tokyo and Calcutta.

That all grades of towns were growing is shown in the following table:

PERCENTAGE URBAN POPULATION: ENGLAND AND WALES

Towns over	1800	1850	1890
10,000	21·30	39·45	61·73
20,000	16·94	35·00	53·58
100,000	9·73	22·58	31·82

Just after mid-century the majority of people in England and Wales lived in towns, by 1901, 77 per cent were urban, by 1951, 80·7 per cent.

The following table shows how the rate of urbanisation differed in other European countries:

PERCENTAGE URBAN POPULATION

	1900	*1910*	*1920*	*1930*	*1950*
France	41·0	44·2	46·4	51·2	52·9
Germany	56·1	61·7	64·6	69·9	71·0
Sweden	21·5	24·8	29·5	38·4	56·3
Spain	32·2	34·8	38·4	42·6	60·5
Bulgaria	19·8	19·1	19·9	21·4	24·6

In most European countries a high degree of urbanisation is a recent phenomenon. Apart from England and Wales, Germany is the only country in which the majority of the population was urban before 1900, though France was approaching it. These were the industrial countries where the industrial revolution, although later than in Britain, greatly accelerated the process. Sweden was predominantly agricultural until the last two decades: the industrial revolution when it reached the Scandinavian countries had considerably changed its character. But in Eastern Europe there are still countries–like Bulgaria–where the degree of urbanisation is very low, and where the increase in urbanisation in this century has been very gradual.

It is certain that the great industrial towns of the last century or century and a half did not even maintain their population by natural increase. The birth rate was high, though not as high as in the country, and it first began to diminish in the towns; the death rate was very high. In the densely built streets of industrial towns in early Victorian England, where people were packed together in appalling densities, diseases were rife; conditions in early factories aggravated the problem. Epidemics ran riot. But the town was a magnet to country folk, and their migration swelled the numbers. Without it towns would have

M

declined. Later, when the rate of town growth was less, rural migration still accounted for increases, for by now better medical services and the conquest of disease was balanced by an ever-decreasing urban birth rate.

Urbanisation is a very recent phenomenon in newer countries. In Canada in 1901 only 37·5 per cent of the population was urban, in 1961, 69·6 per cent. The figures are remarkably similar in Argentina, which in 1905 had 37·4 per cent of its population living in towns, and in 1947, 62·5 per cent. But the processes are not, of course, as closely identified with industrialisation as they were in Europe. There is a closer parallel in the United States.

PERCENTAGE OF URBAN POPULATION IN THE UNITED STATES

1790	5·1	1850	15·3	1910	45·7
1800	6·1	1860	19·8	1920	51·2
1810	7·3	1870	27·5	1930	56·2
1820	7·2	1880	28·2	1940	56·5
1830	8·8	1890	35·1	1950	59·0
1840	10·8	1900	39·7	1950	64·0
				1960	69·9

The United States became predominantly urban only in the decade 1910–20, before which the climb had been gradual, accelerating only in the last two decades of the 19th century. An enormous fillip seems to have been given to the process of urbanisation by the Civil War (though one should be careful of census statistics in the period immediately after it), but it was in the north-east that urban growth was increasing most rapidly. In the period following this came the new migrations from Europe, and these undoubtedly contributed to town growth. It is a common enough observation that European peasantry were translating themselves directly into New World town and city dwellers; this is only a wider aspect of the rural–urban migration which had contributed so much to town growth in Europe. Some demographers in the United States insist that the high rate of natural increase far outweighs rural–urban migration; this may well be, because the worse features of the high urban death rate have been removed since the end of the 19th century by better medical services, better water supply, more food and greater prosperity. The decreasing rate of urbanisation since 1930 may be largely the result of the method of defining urban centres. During this period suburbanisation has been characteristic, and cities and towns everywhere have far outstripped their political boundaries. The extent of this is shown in the table by the second figure for 1950 which includes densely settled urban fringes surrounding cities of 50,000 and over. The 1960 figure also includes these suburban areas.

On the whole urbanisation is still very low in Asia. Only two countries compare with Europe in urbanisation – Israel and Bahrein; and both for very special reasons. Israel's population in the last thirty years has been drawn from Europe's cities. In Bahrein towns have appeared where previously urban life was totally absent, partly to meet the needs of Western technicians and their families. Even in Japan rapid increase has been very recent. In 1921 the percentage urban was only 18·1 and had risen to a modest 37·5 by 1950. But in the following decade there was a massive increase to 63·5 per cent in 1960.

It was even lower in India. In 1881 urban population was only 9·3 per cent of the total, increasing to 10·0 per cent in 1901, but decreasing again to 9·4 per cent in 1911, a feature accounted for by plague and a high urban death rate accompanied by the evacuation of some cities. In 1941 it was 12·8 per cent, but this rose to 18·0 per cent by 1960. In spite of its large cities, India is a land of villages. This is a reminder that the presence of large towns – and their growth – is no index of urbanisation. More than four out of every five Indians live on the land. Indian cities in the past have had little of the industrial-commercial character of West European cities. Many have been political and military, the capitals of rulers who moved their courts frequently. Other cities have thrived as religious centres, the foci of vast pilgrimages.

Even today the character of most Indian cities is not as clear cut as those of Western Europe, and urban and rural characteristics tend to merge. Most cities and towns still have many people employed in agriculture, sometimes as many as ten per cent of the total population. Even in large cities life is carried on by many much as it was in the villages from which they came–within a limited compass and on a subsistence level. On average only about one in three is engaged in industry, and town manufacturing is still on the level of the craftsman in his workshop rather than the operative in a mill. Even in highly industrialised Howrah the vast majority of industrial workers are in workshops employing less than twenty persons.

All classes of towns in India have shown increases in growth in the last 80 years: town growth goes on although urbanisation ncreases so slowly. Usually, the larger the town the faster the rate of growth. The *rate* of growth of towns under 10,000 has actually declined, that of towns between 10,000 and 50,000 increased, and over half a million, markedly increased. In the largest cities, however, there was a decline in the rate of growth between 1951 and 1961. For example, Calcutta increased by only 8·5 per cent, the smallest figure for forty years. Bombay increased by 40 per cent compared with 76 per cent in the previous decade: Madras 23 per cent compared with 65 per cent, and Delhi 85 per cent compared with 94 per cent. But between them these four cities have 11 million people, so the increase is massive enough. Increase in urbanisation in India cannot be accounted for by natural increase. The birth rate in cities is lower than in the country, and the death rate is higher. Again the answer is migration, which in some cities is startlingly high. 67 per cent of the population of Bombay were from outside the city. For Delhi the figure is 49 per cent, for Calcutta, 42 per cent and for Madras 37 per cent. The vast majority came from rural districts, which increases the problems of coming to terms with life in a city. Moreover, men migrants far outnumber women–more than double the number in Calcutta, and almost double in Bombay. This further aggravates social problems.

There is no necessary connection between the growths of large cities and the growth of urbanisation. In Europe there was a period of marked urbanisation in medieval times, but this was followed mainly by a period of urban growth—the appearance of large cities irrespective of whether rural population was increasing or not. The 19th century saw a tremendous spate of urbanisation plus the growth of cities. In India, until very recently, there had been great urban growth, but against a purely peasant background, and the same is true in China. The growth of the very large city—and, for convenience only, geographers tend to take a million population as a symbol of the very large city—is comparatively recent, particularly in intertropical lands.

It has already been mentioned that Paris and London were the only 'million' cities in the world in 1850, and that by 1900 there were 11 (6 in Europe, including European Russia). By the 1920's there were about 20, by 1940, 51, by 1955, 69, and by 1968 this had risen to 130. The 'million' cities of the 1900's were interesting phenomena, those of today are important, because they now contain over 7·66 per cent of the world population. One person in thirteen lives in a city of over a million people. Statistics make precise numbers difficult, but it is probable that in 1968 there were 34 'million' cities in Europe including Russia, 32 in North America, 45 in Asia excluding Russia and 13 in Latin America.

The most interesting phenomenon in the world distribution of these cities is the change in mean latitude (Fig. 8.2). In a mere decade the number of 'million' cities in the tropics has risen from 4 to 23. The same kind of shift is true for cities over 100,000. Moreover, the greatest increases in size occur in cities nearer the equator. European major cities have increased very little—some have actually declined; mid-latitude cities in the new countries have shown increases between 50 per cent and 80 per cent, but those whose mean latitude is 32° have increased between 2 and 3 times; around 23°, 3 and 4 times; and those nearest the equator, 5 times. Saigon (11°) has increased 15·8 times in two decades.

Great though this change is, the tropics are still only slightly urbanised. This latest phenomenon is the growth of massive cities in countries still predominantly agricultural. In the 'new' countries this can be explained, for the large city is the stamp

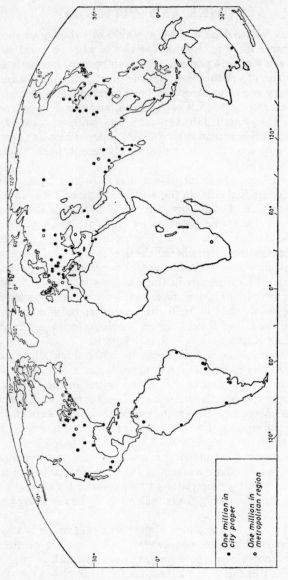

Fig. 8.2. Distribution of major cities.

of an already urbanised homeland. If white settlement is comparatively late, then it depends on the nature and number of indigenous people whether city growth and urbanisation coincide. In Australia most of the settlement has been urban. In South Africa a high degree of urbanisation among the white population is masked by a predominantly rural black population.

SUGGESTIONS FOR FURTHER READING

R. E. DICKINSON: *The West European City* (Routledge and Kegan Paul), 1951.

J. JOHNSON: *Urban Geography* (Pergamon), 1967.

E. JONES: *Towns and Cities* (O.U.P.), 1966.

L. MUMFORD: *The City in History* (Secker and Warburg), 1961.

Chapter 9

TOWNS AND CITIES (2)

9.1 SITES

There are many aspects of towns to excite the curiosity of a
human geographer. First and foremost is the relationship
between the town and the countryside around, the immediate
surroundings and the wider regional setting; secondly, town
also has its own regions and often proves to be a world in
itself.

Site must be one of the first aspects to investigate. Local
topography may have been exploited to find an ideal defensive
site; subsoils and geology may have been taken into consideration, or the presence of water, or nearness to routeways; any
of these—and many more aspects—may have decided builders
of towns in their choice of site. Yet, however vital these elements may have been in deciding the site of an individual
town, siting is not a subject upon which we can generalise
easily. One point of view only would warrant such generalisations. If we believed that the site alone dictated the presence
or absence of a town then we might be justified in talking
about, for example, 'hilltop towns' as if the site determined the
town. In fact that term is merely descriptive; it tells us where
the towns are, but as they may be there for many different
reasons it does not add much to our knowledge. That there is
a town at a certain point is not necessarily and wholly due to
the site factors at that point, but to a much wider set of circumstances. In other words, a given area of land may have many
sites for any number of towns but this does not mean that a
town will arise on every suitable site. A site only becomes significant when it is chosen. On the other hand, if the situation
demands it a town or city will grow up on what appears to be
a very poor site indeed. The value of sites varies with the way
in which people use them. Sites which appear ideal to one

TOWNS AND CITIES (2)   181

society may lose their appeal to another. The pueblos of
Arizona may seem to us to be on such obviously good sites that
we have to remind ourselves that the Hopi moved up to these
mesa tops from the plateau floor in historic times for defensive
purposes: this was a response to the needs of the society, and
such an important one that it outweighed the inconvenience
of the water supply and the cultivated fields being at the base
of the mesa.

Each site, then, must be evaluated carefully according to
the situation when the town was built. The situation will probably change with time, but a town site does not always reflect
this change. A hill town built in times of war remains so, long
after the dangers of wars have passed. But a town's development will always reflect historical changes. However much a
geographer may rhapsodise on the site of New York in relation
to the Hudson–Mohawk gap, it was a small town indeed until
that gap had been cleared of Indians, and penetrated by
Americans, and until the possibility of expansion beyond the
gap gradually became a reality.

In addition to site the geographer is also interested in the
morphology of the town. In attempting any kind of generalisation on morphology this account will first confine itself to the
Western European town.

9.2 HISTORIC PATTERNS OF THE WESTERN CITY

In the last chapter the stages in the development of the
Western European town were outlined; they were: Roman,
medieval, renaissance, industrial and modern. Many cities
reflect all these stages in their plan, and it is surprising how
many of the stages survive in most. Even when original buildings have long disappeared, the width of a street, its direction,
its relationship to other streets, all these will have fossilised the
city of hundreds of years ago.

Plans of medieval towns, or medieval centres of today's
towns, reveal no love of symmetry (Fig. 9.1). If the town was
consciously planned, as many bastide towns were, it will have
a rough symmetry, but more often it is a haphazard collection of narrow streets, for usually the line of the street will be

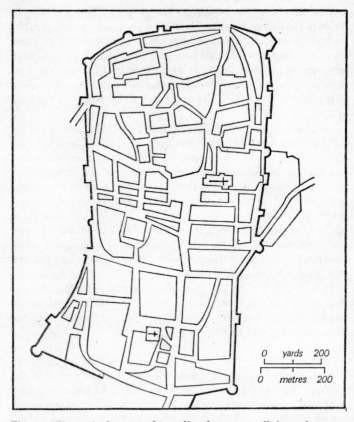

Fig. 9.1. The main features of a medieval town—wall, irregular street pattern, central market place and church—are all shown in Langres in eastern France.

determined by the frontage of houses. But in addition there are three fundamental features which are common to all medieval towns, and to their relicts today. The first is the wall, the protection against enemies. The medieval town was strictly confined within this limit, and often this limitation led to crowded conditions, with houses rising high above the streets as in

Edinburgh. Yet there were houses outside some town walls. These were the *suburbs*–so named on Speed's early 17th-century county maps of England and Wales–the *faubourgs* of European towns. The suburb was particularly characteristic of medieval towns established in alien territory: Edward I's planned fortress towns of North Wales, Caernarvon and Conway, had well-defined suburbs, for the Welsh were kept outside the walls by their English conquerors. This was not only an interesting morphological feature, but an important social one, and reference to this will be made later. Most medieval cities remained small, but some which grew rapidly found that they had to rebuild the walls time and time again, a reflection of continuing insecurity during rapid growth.

The second conspicuous feature of the medieval town was an open space near the centre where the market was held. These irregular spaces have often been preserved, though most markets have now ceased to occupy streets and squares. Often near the market was the town hall, and sometimes the elaborately built headquarters of the guilds of merchants and craftsmen.

The third feature was the church which usually dominated the medieval town just as the church organisation dominated the life of the people. Many of these churches remain as a priceless heritage. To a large extent the church had been responsible for preserving many of the best things of civilisation during the eclipse of the town in the Dark Ages. Now it emerged triumphant. The church was the monumental successor to the pyramid and the temple, the symbol both of the wealth of the community and its singlemindedness; the surplus of time and the surplus of energy are clearly attested in the Gothic masterpieces of this age of cathedrals. Old St. Paul's dominated the medieval skyline of London; Durham cathedral still dominates its defensive hill.

The next stage in growth coincides with the renaissance, and also with the consolidation of the small principalities of medieval Europe and the emergence of larger states. This is the period of the growth of the capital city. London, by the end of the 18th century, had a population of over 800,000,

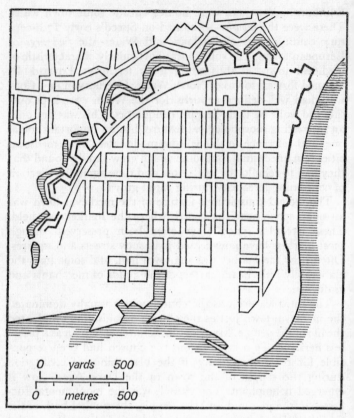

Fig. 9.2. Frederica in Denmark shows the orderly planning and elaborate defences of the early renaissance period.

though the other towns of England had not grown so appreciably beyond their medieval confines. The first clear difference in plan in the earliest stage of the renaissance town is the replacement of the defensive wall by an elaborate system of ditches and ramparts (Fig. 9.2). This was a gradual response to the introduction of gunpowder and artillery, and the aim seemed to be to keep the enemy as far away as possible. But the striking characteristic of the new defences is the precision of their execution. Plans of new towns and fortresses of this period look like exquisitely designed stars, the precisely drawn salients introducing an orderliness which reflected the beginnings of scientific exactitude in learning. Naarden in Holland is a fine example of a town which developed no farther—indeed this new system of defence was more of a straitjacket than the old—but many cities, like Copenhagen, owe an inner 'green belt' to this system, a circle of parkland still containing the mounds and the remnants of the watercourse which were once the city's defences.

Inside the later renaissance city the street pattern became transformed. Again the mathematical regularity is striking, but the dominant element is the avenue, very wide and long and perfectly straight. This was called by architects 'the military' street, and indeed it could and did facilitate the easy movement of troops and wheeled vehicles. In more settled times it also became a parade, and later still its shops took over the functions of the old market place.

The monumental building of this phase was the palace, a sure reflection of the way in which capital cities controlled the wealth of a state. This was emphasised because here too was the home of the head of the state. Versailles is a notable example, with its radiating avenues and immense palace. Even more spectacular in plan is Karlsruhe, where there are six radiating avenues leading to the palace, although few of these have been built upon. The plan for a 17th-century palace in Whitehall in London failed to materialise beyond the Banqueting Hall, which can still be seen, but the Naval College at Greenwich is a good example of the scale and planning of these monuments. Around the palace were accumulated other symbols of wealth and leisure—art galleries, theatres, pleasure gardens and, eventually, museums. In terms of domestic architecture, the later renaissance period has given us squares and terraces and crescents; Bloomsbury and the squares of the West End of London, Bath, Cheltenham and Brighton all echo this late phase. Just as the plans were formal and geometric, so the architecture was invariably classical in style.

The industrial stage witnessed an increase in urbanisation and town growth which has already been referred to, against a background of the use of coal and iron on a new, vast scale. One of the technical changes of the industrial revolution must be mentioned because it gave rise to such concentrations of population. Motive power in previous eras had been supplied by water and wind, and the unit of power, the mill, was small. This had meant a scatter of small manufacture. The countryside had its mills: the city had its workshops: but they never obtruded, let alone dictated the plan and growth. The steam engine radically changed this. Here was a power unit capable of working many machines. Indeed, the bigger the unit the more economical, so that one unit might give work to hundreds of people at a single site. In the early 19th century in Britain, factories were being built to employ 500 persons; each time a factory was opened the population of a small town was being concentrated at one point. What were the features of the new towns which suddenly appeared, and the extensions of the older towns?

The predominant impression of the industrial town is overall lack of plan and repetition in detail: the repetition reflects the regularity of the machine (Fig. 9.3). Uniformity replaces the unity in design of the former stage. The immense crowding of industrial centres in the first half of the 19th century in England and Wales led to deplorable living conditions in crowded tenements and back-to-back houses (some of which still exist) in narrow courts. This was offset to some extent by mid-century by-laws which demanded certain minimum standards in size of house, height of rooms and width of street, for example. The outcome of these by-laws was the machine-like repetition of minimum standard houses which we have inherited from Victorian times. Streets became a standard size, with no discrimination for those taking wheeled traffic and those taking pedestrians. There was no planning and no sorting out of functions: streets of houses and factories stood side by side. The over-all impression is of mechanical standardisation. Middle-class houses were very narrow, but taller and much deeper; for the value of frontage was beginning to be appreciated and pressure on urban land was beginning to tell.

But the period which witnessed the massing of the industrial workers in towns also witnessed the beginning of the with-drawal from the town centre of the upper and middle class and the beginning of suburbia in the modern sense. Richer people withdrew to pleasanter and unspoilt areas, away from factories and smoke, to land beyond the town where land

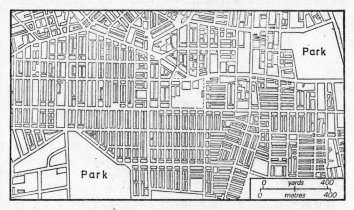

Fig. 9.3. The monotonous repetition of industrial housing in Manchester.

values permitted parks and large gardens; this too is typical of the city pattern in the industrial phase.

The monumental buildings of this period offer a strange contrast to those of the past. The successors of church and palace are often Workmen's Halls and Mechanics' Institutes; and in many small industrial towns these buildings are often in striking contrast to all others. But the real monuments of this period are the factories, warehouses, gas holders and-above all-the railway stations of our larger cities. In London, for example, the railway inspired new forms in new materials, though these wonderful iron vaults which span the platforms are often hidden by more convential façades. Railway stations, incidentally, often mark the limits of the renaissance town and the beginning of the industrial zone. Georgian London is ringed with great stations, and immediately beyond them begins the monotonous pattern of industrial houses.

In the industrial phase, railways brought people into towns; subsequently new modes of transport have been taking people away from town centres, to create modern suburbs. The building of mill houses in the 19th century allowed the worker to be near his work. Public transport since 1900 has worked a transformation in making it easy to live elsewhere until now the worker can 'work anywhere and live nowhere'. Tramcars initiated the change; it was continued by buses and now, increasingly, by private cars. This ease of movement, together with the increasing improvement of physical living conditions, such as bigger gardens, has meant a much lighter density of houses and people. The greater part of the suburban movement of the 20th century is an extension of the earlier, but vastly increased by more and more people from lower income groups. So the suburban villa gave way to the modern semi-detached, and the vast garden to a diminutive lawn, while the reaction against regimented uniformity led to a chaotic individualism. The rehousing of lower-income groups by urban councils between the wars led to considerable suburban expansions. While middle-class suburbs led to lack of form, council estates have shown a variety of geometric designs which, until recently, however, have lacked focus because they consisted of nothing but masses of houses. They are easily recognised on a map: as a physical environment they were incomparably better than anything that had been built before, but the emphasis on the need of the single family is very apparent.

The latest stage in the development of the Western European city has seen attempts to provide an environment for society, rather than for industrial families, and groups of houses are now often focussed on communal activities. This is best expressed in the neighbourhoods of new towns in Britain. Each neighbourhood, of about 10,000 people, is grouped round a shopping parade, church, school and playing fields.

Monumental architecture is difficult to find in 20th-century towns. The individualism that ran riot in the suburbs was the antithesis of the conditions which produced the monuments of the past. But it is perhaps significant that in post-war years schools are the bases of neighbourhoods and the focus of neighbourhood life, and are often striking contributions to 20th-century architecture.

9.3 THE MODERN WESTERN CITY

We have been looking at the urban forms which each phase in the history of the Western European city has produced. Within many the progression from medieval core, through renaissance squares and industrial zones to modern suburbs shows all these phases: some include the latest phase of all – the throwing off of satellite towns. But the picture is incomplete without mention of the rebuilding of most centres to give us the city cores of today. Here building is usually on a larger scale than ever before, increasing congestion until the centre is choked with traffic and people. Many European cities are reluctant to build upwards in the city centre. Until very recently Paris limited new buildings to eight stories, and London's modest skyline is only gradually being broken by tall office blocks in spite of the enormous pressure on the land. The first real skyscraper in Europe was the recent 127 m/417 ft high Pirelli building in Milan, a very modest block compared with downtown New York. The type of building which is now being erected is the slab block, the shape which gives the greatest floor space in relation to circulation space. The increasing concentration of tall buildings, the vast majority of which are office blocks, is a reflection of the increase in services and administration: these buildings may well be the monuments of today's European city, as they are of the American city since the beginning of the century.

The great congestion which results from the building of these large blocks is posing almost insuperable problems. But gradually new city forms are evolving which might meet mid-20th-century needs. The use of different levels was thought of half a century and more ago, by the underground railway

N

system in London and the elevated railways in Chicago, but private transport is proving more difficult. In Europe super-highways (such as those in Brussels and Stockholm) are one answer, and the idea of separating motor and pedestrian traffic is gaining ground. This will result in more extensive pedestrian precincts, already a distinctive feature of the re-built cities of Coventry and Rotterdam.

The historical growth described above results in purely morphological patterns. Equally important is the functional pattern: for the work of a large city usually sorts itself out, giving rise to different sectors devoted to different functions. One of the prime functions of the town is still marketing, and, as always, selling and buying is concentrated near the centre. With the growth of a great city a former medieval centre may be taken over almost entirely by shops and markets, and eventually rebuilt. Sometimes the plan is medieval and the profile modern. The market is at the crossroads, not only of the city but of the region beyond; this is the point which is most accessible to the greatest number of people. This need for accessibility is particularly evident in specialised shops or multiple stores, of which there are very few even in large towns: a central site is deemed almost essential for these. For the same reasons banks will seek central sites. Similarly, hotels are usually near the centre as well as certain administrative offices and centres of social services. In a larger city the busi-ness and shopping centres may well be separate, though both will be central. London, for example, has a twin centre in its City and West End; New York has a Mid Town shopping area and a Down Town business area around Wall Street. Beyond the immediate centre the shops and offices will often have spread to the former residential areas of squares and terraces, sometimes without rebuilding. Many fine Georgian squares have their quota of small shops and offices, and often uni-versity buildings will be found here; Bloomsbury in London is a good example.

The industrial sector of the city is usually a part of the 19th-century expansion. Here by-law houses are indiscriminately mixed with factories, although often industry is concentrated along rivers, canals and railways. 20th-century houses tend to form purely residential zones around the city, where land values fall as one goes farther outward.

These functional zones have grown rather haphazardly but they tie up with the age of different parts of the city: the re-built centre, the old, former residential zone just beyond this, the industrial 19th-century zone next, and the new residential areas on the periphery, to give a widely recognised pattern which would recur in most Western European type cities.

These generalisations are not necessarily valid for towns and cities elsewhere. It is true that the European concept of a city has spread over much of the earth's surface. In North America, Australia, South Africa and parts of South America an urban civilisation is found which was transferred from Europe, and one would expect great similarities up to a certain point. The early core is missing of course and most of the towns were platted before they were built-up; though many South American cities had irregular cores, Manhattan south of Wall Street still shows the irregular pattern of the 17th century, and so does central Boston. But the dominant plan of New World cities is the grid: not so much the result of inspired planning as in the renaissance towns in Europe, but because this was the most convenient way to plot new land (Fig. 9.4). Indeed, the avenues and crescents of renaissance planning are con-spicuously absent. Washington, D.C., is one of the outstanding exceptions in the United States, a basic grid system being over-laid by radiating avenues and by a functional axis: which is a true reflection of 18th-century European ideas. The majority of New World cities have the unrelieved grid only, which has more in common with the mechanical and repetitive order-liness of the industrial cities of Europe. This is acceptable – though monotonous – on a level terrain, as in Chicago, but less so when draped uncompromisingly over the hills of San Francisco, where the ignoring of contours results in so many precipitous streets. In this grid pattern there was no concession to different land use, and consequently there is no hint of functional differentiations on the plan. But the blocks devel-oped very differently: there is nothing more striking, or more

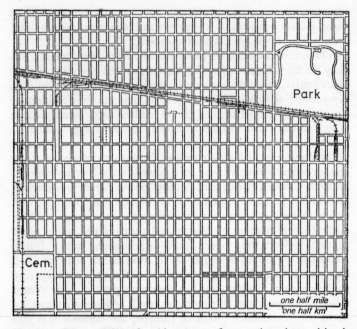

Fig. 9.4. The unrelieved grid system of most American cities is exemplified in this part of Chicago.

typical of the New World city, than the differences in profile between the great concentration of building in the centre and the low skyline of the residential area beyond. The skyscraper core is characteristic. It is usually very restricted in area–in Chicago it is confined within the Loop, i.e. the inner circle of the elevated railway, in New York to parts only of Manhattan –but it is almost unrestricted in height. Movement in these cores has changed direction: people travel greater distances up and down by lifts than they do to and fro: and faster, for road traffic decreases in speed with increasing congestion.

It is this congestion which leads to an interesting revaluation of the accepted form and pattern of the city in Europe and in the New World. The accepted form was based on accessibility, and who can say that the centre of a city like New York is easily accessible? The attempts to limit the duration of car parking in London lead to a reduction in accessibility. Yet most of the city's central functions have arisen from the need for accessibility. If accessibility is tied to the car, an assumption one can take for granted in the United States, if not yet in Britain, a place is said to be accessible if it can be approached by a car, and a car is the least welcomed item in a crowded city centre. Consequently some functions are dispersing. This began in the United States with motels, which clustered around roads leading to the city centre, but kept well outside the city. This means that one traditionally central function is now peripheral: travellers–and their cars–are accommodated before they come into the city. Again, in order to solve the parking problem–i.e. to make for greater accessibility–super-markets and shopping parades began to appear outside city limits, where parking was unlimited and land very cheap. This has reached its logical conclusion in some shopping areas being located equidistant from several towns. The point of greatest accessibility, paradoxically, is outside the city–and one must consider seriously whether the growth of the city along tradi-tional lines has not in many ways strangled the city and whether we will now be forced to accept radical departures in new planned towns.

Some cities in Latin America, e.g. Sao Paulo, are typically Western, but others have very different features. For example, in Rio de Janeiro the inner, older areas are still residential, and very poor slum areas can exist side by side with them, possibly because high walls make each large house self-con-tained. But the most striking feature of this city is the slum property on the hillsides above the town, where the mud huts of squatter settlements, lacking services or paved streets, is the very antithesis of the Western European city, where on com-parable sites one would expect upper-class suburbs.

9.4 PRE-INDUSTRIAL CITIES

Eastern cities are different in kind, for they reflect rather different functions and a different history. Although a great city like Chungking has many basic similarities to a Western European city, the differences are marked (Fig. 9.5). The city, which is very old, rebuilt its walls in 1370, 1644 and 1760, and until the 1920's was contained within them. Later developments have shared many features with the West, but inside the walls the main impression is of a great density of building and a lack of street plan. The main thoroughfares are predominantly

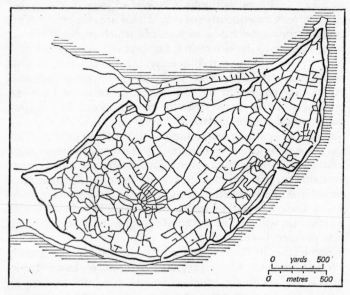

Fig. 9.5. The wall and the irregular street pattern of old Chunking is typical of the pre-industrial oriental city.

east–west, following the contour, and many connecting 'streets' are nothing more than steep flights of steps: there is no recognisable pattern. Congestion is more marked because growth within the walls eliminated streets rather than encouraged high buildings. There is a distinction between the west and south, where streets were lined with the high walls of upper-class houses, and the remainder, where streets were lined with small shops which spilled onto the roadway.

It has been suggested that there are elements in this basic to all Asiatic cities which have grown within the framework of agricultural empires. They are: the wall, the lack of plan, and the two basic social elements which are reflected in the detailed morphology and function, namely the upper princely/aristocratic class and the artisan/merchant class. Certainly old Indian cities would show parallels, complicated by segregation of castes which had different standards of living.

Departures from this basic pattern – or lack of pattern – are largely the outcome of subsequent history and contact with the West. In many Chinese ports the *bund* was introduced by Western merchants; this is a complex of docks, a skirting highway, banks, warehouses and offices, which has become a commercial centre. In Singapore and Shanghai, for example, the *bund* has now become a true Western-type core, and skyscrapers are common.

In India the cantonment, a relic of the 18th century, presents novel patterns. These are the so-called *lines*, civil lines, for example, where Europeans were quartered, and coolie lines. This sector was often separated from the native city, or outside its walls, and there could be no greater contrast than between its regimented orderliness and low density, and the chaotic and crowded native city (Fig. 9.6). Inside the Indian city the distribution of functions are rather different from those of a Western European city. There is no concentrated commercial core, but rather a series of dispersed market and commercial centres, and high-class houses are often near the centre and not on the outskirts. In the last three decades many cities have developed industrial sectors, and factories and their associated houses are diversifying the traditional pattern considerably. In many Indian cities the latest phase in expansion is incongruously European, often suburban patterns which faintly echo interwar Europe. But post-partition planning for resettlement has sometimes been on a large scale, culminating in the very fine grid plan of Chandrigarh, capital of Indian Punjab. Again the contrast with the native pattern, in form and in functional zoning, is very striking.

Perhaps the farthest removed from our ideas of what a town

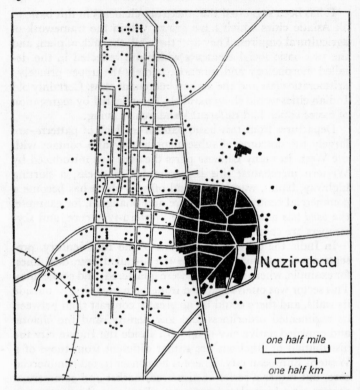

Fig. 9.6. There are marked contrasts between the regular pattern and very light density of the European 'lines' of Indian towns and the densely peopled 'native' centres to which they are attached.

should look like is the West African town. Indeed, applying our criteria rigorously we might even doubt that we are dealing with towns at all. Their greatest claim to urbanism is size for many exceed 50,000, some 100,000; functionally any permanent settlement which has a chief is a town. Yet in aspect they are more like villages, and the vast majority of their people are peasants.

They have a long history, some as trade centres on caravan

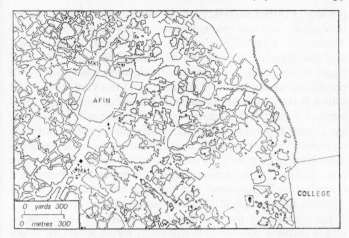

Fig. 9.7. In Nigerian towns, 'roads' are merely spaces between compounds. The chief's compound (Afin) is central, and so are the markets. Remains of the wall can still be seen (Oyo, Western Region).

routes, but only recently have European ideas and styles of administration, mining and commerce been introduced. Morphologically the town is like an unplanned village where street patterns are absent, where there is no great variation in size of houses, and where functions like shopping and handcraft are dispersed throughout and have no great effect on urban forms (Fig. 9.7).

9.5 CLASSIFICATION OF WESTERN CITIES

Faced with so many towns and cities, so different in size, form, history and function, a geographer's reaction is to try to introduce order in seeming chaos and suggest a classification. A basic division has already been assumed above, for the main topic was the Western European city, and there are sufficient differences between this and oriental, African, or even some Latin American cities, to warrant this qualification. In so far as cities reflect different cultures, these broad differences are obvious. Further classification demands more thought. Population is an easy and convenient way to group cities and is used universally. The 'million' city seems to be the ultimate class, and one which has been written about frequently. But this figure of one million, together with all other figures on which classifications are based, is arbitrary, and not very meaningful unless it shows the importance of a town or implies its functions or status; and as these elements correspond to different sizes under different conditions in different countries, numbers can never be more than the most obvious and easiest classification. If we believe that the most important thing about a town is its function, then we could take a further step and suggest a classification by function; and this is generally acceptable for Western European and North American towns.

Even confining the functional classification to one type of city it involves considerable difficulty, for although all towns are centres of exchange, the vast majority also have a variety of functions in addition. Most towns specialise, and it is this degree of specialisation which places a town in a certain class. In Britain, for example, Crewe and Swindon are automatically coupled in our minds with railways–they are transport towns. Equally obvious, Eastbourne and Bournemouth are resorts, and Birmingham is an industrial city. There is no difficulty here in pinpointing the activity of greatest importance. But many towns are borderline cases, and methods of classification must be checked against employment or occupational figures. Nor is it even then simply a matter of looking for the industry which employs most people. Employment in such things as retail shopping–common to all towns–must be largely discounted, other classes must be selected carefully, and the significance of certain critical percentages argued.

An American classification suggests the following kinds of towns: manufacturing, retail, wholesale, diversified, transport, mining, learning, resorts, political. On this basis nearly half the towns in the United States are manufacturing, and they are concentrated in the north-east, as one would expect; retail centres lie outside this area, for they are the towns which have no greatly specialised functions, except regionally, and half of

them are between 95° W. and 100° W. Wholesale centres in
the west are large cities often concerned with packing agricultural produce. 18 transport centres are railroad towns and
14 ports. Only 14 are classed as mining towns (10 of these are
coalmining centres), and there are 17 university towns, mainly
mid-west and prairie towns dominated by a campus. The few
resorts show a marked preference for Florida and the dry hot
south-west. There is only one wholly political centre and that
is Washington, D.C. Here employed persons fall into roughly
two classes: those who are federal officials and those who serve
them in various capacities. A similar classification could be
applied in Britain or in Western Europe generally.

One must be careful to accept such a classification for what
it is worth and not read too much into it. Its greatest pitfall is
to forget that each town can be counted only *once*. New York
or London, for example, must be put into one class only,
although they are in fact more important in most other functions than even those towns specialising in such functions. New
York and Chicago are much more important as university
towns than most of those classified as centres of learning in the
United States; in the same way Glasgow is a more important
university centre than St. Andrews although the latter is a
university town. And although in London administration and
government are so important, they vie with the equally important industrial and port functions. Many towns are centres
of government, very few emerge as purely political centres, e.g.
Washington and Canberra.

Outside Europe, North America and Australasia, many of
these classes mean little. Of the 27 cities of Asia which had
passed the one million mark in 1960, 9 (Cairo, Baghdad,
Lahore, Delhi, Nanking, Canton, Peking, Hankow and Kyoto)
are agricultural, i.e. they belong to an agricultural background,
and have few of the elements which decide the class of Western
towns. The great towns of West Africa, of course, are also
agricultural. Many other oriental cities have flourished by
trade, and 7 of the one million cities have had a mercantile
fillip from the West. But perhaps the most significant trend in
the larger cities of the East is the development of industry and

of increasing administration, and it is likely that such cities will eventually become more like their counterparts in the West.

9.6 POPULATION STRUCTURE IN CITIES

The last chapter showed the Western city to have been a gradually evolving man-made landscape, the differences in forms within it reflecting changes in techniques and society at various stages in its growth. But it would be an over-simplification to suppose that history had mechanically produced these different urban patterns, for at any one stage different groups in society made different demands which were met in a variety of ways. At every stage there were rich and poor, master and servant. Town society has by its very nature always been complex, and this complexity cannot be disassociated from urban landscape differences. Without people the town is meaningless –a mere pattern on a map. Colour, character, life itself is given by the town folk. Children and noise are part of a working-class estate, crowds and traffic of a city centre at midday, peace and quiet of an upper-class suburb. Here we will be concerned with some of the details of differentiation within towns and the way in which they are intimately bound up with contrasts between groups within urban society.

Although towns generally have a very high density of population compared with rural areas, there are great variations of density within any one town. In Belfast, a fairly typical example of a major industrial city, net density per sq. km (i.e. number of persons per sq. km of land occupied by gardens and roads and services leading to them) varies from 69,000 to 124. These variations are not haphazard, for the heavy densities are in the industrial areas of 19th-century by-law houses, and the light in the upper-class residential areas. Density is tied, not only to class, but partly to the age of houses, for modern council estates have light densities. This general pattern of densities is repeated in all industrial cities in Britain. Another common feature is the empty city centre, that area which has been rebuilt as shops and offices, and which now permanently houses only an hotel population, and a few caretakers.

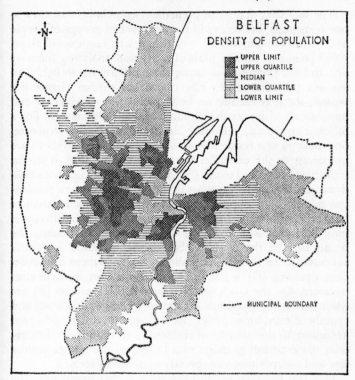

Fig. 9.8. Density of population in Belfast by enumeration districts.
Upper limit 69,000; upper quartile 35,000; median 24,000; lower quartile 9,500; lower limit 124 per square kilometre.

All these density figures relate, of course, to places of residence, and this is the picture of a city at night. We have no density map of a city at noon, but it would be very different—the centre choked with people and the residential areas partly denuded. Between 8 and 9 in the morning and 5 and 6 in the afternoon the whole population is in flux. It is necessary to remind ourselves of this fact because mapping the density of population may produce too static a picture. Movement and change are the very essence of city life.

The fact that density of permanent households can vary so much suggests differences in the structure of groups of people and the way in which they live. Taking small samples of about 2,000 people in various parts of a city and analysing them by age and sex is enough to bring these differences to light. An age–sex pyramid of any city centre has neither rhyme nor reason, for it is mainly an hotel population – accidental and haphazard, with very few children and few old persons. For a 'normal' pyramid, reflecting the standard family structure, one must go to a residential area: but even here variations are numerous as the examples from Belfast show (Fig. 9.9). An industrial residential sector (H) has a wide base – i.e. more children – and a gradual tapering in the old age groups: a residential middle- and upper-class area (V) has a much narrower base but a pronounced middle-age 'spread'. Further differences may be introduced by religious differences: in Belfast, the broad base of the working-class district pyramid is greatly accentuated in Roman Catholic areas (D), where a middle-class pyramid (G) is not unlike the Protestant working-class pyramid. On the city's outskirts new housing estates (F) are distinguished by pyramids with grossly exaggerated bases and rapidly diminishing peaks, for houses are often allocated according to the number of children in the family, and rarely does space permit grandparents to live on the estate. Family size and composition vary greatly in different sectors.

One last example worth examining is that found near the city centre in Belfast (T). It is distinguished by a preponderance of men and women between 20 and 30, by comparatively few children, and more than one would expect in late middle age and old age, particularly of women. These are the characteristics of a 'rooming' district. The example shown lies very near a university, and there is a high proportion of students living in flatlets and rooms; there is also a high percentage of office workers and nurses. These groups, though overwhelmingly preponderant, are constantly changing; it is the ageing group, which includes many landladies, which is more or less constant. The connection between this population structure and the kinds of houses in this district is very close indeed. This

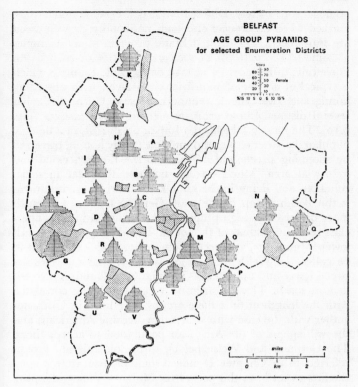

Fig. 9.9. Age/sex pyramids for selected enumeration districts in Belfast.

was a former middle-class residential district of big houses. Modern incomes and lack of domestic help have forced those who have not moved to smaller and newer suburban houses to let their rooms. Such an area, of large, old houses with an unstable population, much of it continually moving, is found near the centre of many large cities.

9.7 ETHNIC GROUPS IN CITIES

Differences so far discussed – of density, age and sex, and, by implication, of class and status – are differences within a homogeneous society. Differentiation can become much more marked when differences of colour, nationality or even creed are introduced. The United States provides many examples of some of the patterns of society that arise in such cases. For ethnic differences let us take one specific example which is typical of north-east industrial cities faced with absorbing immigrants over the last hundred years. Utica, N.Y., has several distinct ethnic areas, though none is exclusive (Fig. 9.10). The most marked is the Italian north-east, in a densely populated district of two and multiple family houses, traversed by shopping streets and adjacent to the railway, canal and industrial area. Much smaller, but not dissimilar in social cohesion, and living in the same kind of urban environment, is the Polish group in the west. German families are much more dispersed, a high proportion being found in the upper-class residential areas of the south. The Welsh, though much fewer in numbers, still occupy one sector sufficiently for it to be called the Welsh ward—midway in all characteristics between lower and upper class—but many are found in the residential south. These distributions can be closely correlated with the length of time these groups have lived in Utica, together with the ease with which they became Americans and the willingness of the American population to accept them. The Germans and Welsh belong to the old migrant groups referred to in Chapter 4—indeed some of them were among the first to settle in this part of the Mohawk Valley; the peak of their migration lies in the 1850's and 1860's. Italians and Poles are 'new' immigrants. Many are first generation, i.e. they were born in Italy or Poland. These immigrants, with a background of rural poverty, are poor and unskilled when they arrive, they must live in the cheapest apartments in the oldest parts of the town, under crowded conditions and near the most undesirable sites, such as factories and railways. Being in a strange country there is also a tendency for these groups to be closely knit and for new immigrants to live among their countrymen. Germans and Welsh, who are old migrants, assimilated, acceptable as north-west Europeans and Protestants, have grown with the city and have moved outwards

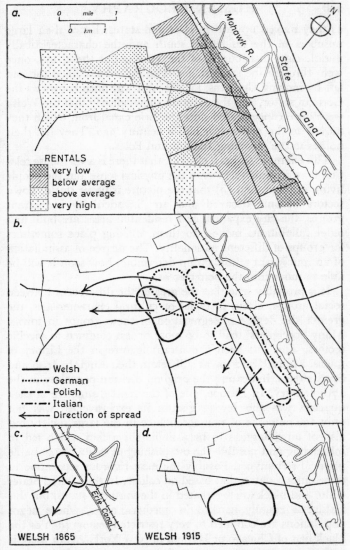

Fig. 9.10. (*a*) The residential zones of Utica, N.Y., shown by rentals. (*b*) Distribution of four ethnic groups in Utica. (*c*) and (*d*) show the movement of Welsh between 1865 and 1915.

as they moved upward in class and status; hence their large numbers in the residential south and the characteristically middle-class distribution of the Welsh. But these, too, once went through the same stages. The Poles have filled the gap left by moving Germans, for the west was once known as the German sector, and the diagram shows clearly that the Welsh were once concentrated near the Erie canal from which they moved to the new sector half a century ago. They left their houses to the incoming Italians and Poles.

This example makes it clear (i) that there is a very close relation between town sectors in the physical sense and the people living in them, and (ii) that the picture is never static. Town sectors become decayed and are 'invaded' by immigrant groups, the city expands, new residential areas are built and older inhabitants move into them, making place sometimes for groups of different nationality. The degree of assimilation of an immigrant ethnic group determines how soon it will be able to move into the better areas.

It is probably true that the greater the differences between social groups, either in racial or cultural characteristics, the greater the degree of segregation of these groups in towns. Many 'foreigners' tend to be more or less confined to specific sectors. This has been a constant feature in the history of towns. Many Ulster towns still retain their English, Irish and Scots streets, indicating the original division of society in the 17th century. In Europe, one of the most distinctive of such quarters was the Jewish ghetto: its exclusiveness was not only the outcome of non-acceptance in the large society but also of unwillingness to be assimilated, a fact which led to inbreeding and possibly the establishing of easily recognisable physical stereotypes. Possibly the most rigorous separation in some cities today is that based on colour. In the United States white and black are segregated in the southern states, but this feature is equally marked in northern cities, where negro populations are confined to very restricted sectors such as the black belt of Chicago or Harlem in New York. Again there is a close correlation between such segregated populations and the urban environment. Many coloured areas were formerly high-class residential areas, from which the former occupants have moved to more desirable and newer suburbs. In these large houses negro families exist at extremely high densities. Density tends to increase because the group is so segregated and expansion is almost impossible. Restrictive clauses in leases and intimidation are two methods of maintaining the position, though if a negro family does succeed in establishing itself outside the belt, then possibly that new block will be deserted by white people and taken over by negroes. The position of the black belt is, then, not accidental: in origin it is like the ethnic belt, but it differs in that movement beyond it is severely restricted, just as acceptance into the society is a rare occurrence to the black person.

9.8 SOCIAL PATTERNS

Change is the great characteristic of the West European city of today. The centre, where rebuilding is more apparent, is continually expanding with city growth and consequently is eating into the oldest part, i.e. the part immediately beyond the centre. Here one finds slum property – a zone of decay. The decay is often social as well as physical, for over-crowding, low standards of living, inadequate sanitation all seem to be conditions in which social ills prevail, and which seem to be the last refuge of those who have failed to find a part to play in society. Slums grow with a town, and until society can erase them altogether they will continue to do so.

There are other regions of great change in cities which do not necessarily result in decay either of property or society. This zone is often farther from the centre than the decayed zone, but is one which is changing its function. This change means that houses sometimes become shops. This is a process common to radial roads and it is easy to distinguish the stages: the unchanged house with a display window added; a whole ground floor added; an entire new frontage – and so on. Between the radial roads which are undergoing this change, former large houses change their functions, sometimes as inconspicuously as into boarding houses in which the social structure changes more radically than the physical. Other large houses become hotels, offices, nursing homes, hostels–all with the minimum of physical change but with a fair retention of physical standards. But it all implies social change. Even when a house is subdivided into flats, the possibility is that it will not house a complete family for long; the couple with children will wish to move into a suburban house with garden at the first opportunity. This, then, is a zone of social change, where the population is transitory or temporary.

We are so familiar with the location of slums and regions of transition near the centre of large cities that it must not be forgotten that though this is a common pattern in the Western European industrial city it is by no means a universal pattern. South American cities are often ringed by slums, occupying those very locations where we might expect the middle- and upper-class suburbs. These slums are rather different: they are shanty towns put up by peasants moving in from the country-side. Many of them eventually replace themselves by decent housing, for they represent a stage in city growth rather than in city decay. In those same cities the wealthy are often found in central areas, in contrast to our own cities where most of those who could afford to have fled to cleaner suburbs. It will be appreciated, then, that what is described here concerns the Western industrial city.

The way in which city sectors–shopping and business centre, decayed property, zone in transition, industrial and residential sectors–seem to be repeated so often and to reflect stages in growth and the effects of age, has tempted some workers to suggest idealised plans which apply–with slight deviations–to all West European cities. It was Professor Burgess of the University of Chicago who first recognised the zones of a city and the intimate interplay of environment and society, and he described, for Chicago, a series of concentric zones which would apply to all cities (Fig. 9.11). First came an inner zone, entirely business and shopping. Around it came what he called the zone of transition (decay), and here were found the under-world, the unstable segments of society, first-generation immi-grants, the bulk of the black belt. Beyond was a zone of work-ing men's homes, less old, more stable in society, housing in

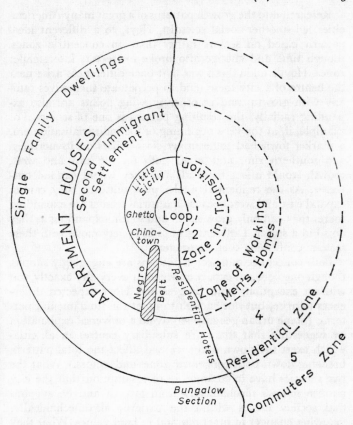

Fig. 9.11. Burgess's zones of the Western city, based on Chicago.

addition second-generation immigrants; for example, Germans. The fourth zone was the suburban zone where the basic stable family was predominant, and beyond this again was a commuters' zone. This zoning reflects the process of ageing, decay and change characteristic of a growing city. What is less acceptable in Burgess's ideas is the too mechanical way in which social groups move within this framework—almost willy-nilly.

Research into the growth patterns of a great many American cities led another social scientist, Hoyt, to a different ideal pattern based on sectors rather than on concentric zones, though time and change also broke his sectors into smaller zones. Hoyt's main thesis was that once differences arise near the centre of a city these tend to perpetuate themselves radially with growth, and as other growing points are also expanding radially, the resulting pattern is one of sectors. For example, if, at the very beginning of the industrialisation era, a market town had some upper-class houses on its northern and southern rim, and small mills on the east and west, growth would affect them all and they would expand outwards. As the residential nuclei push outward they cannot expand east and west because industrial sectors are expanding there; they can only grow north and south, expanding as they do so in a sector. Different groups in society move with these sectors, confirming their character.

Both concentric and sector patterns are engagingly simple, though one does not expect either to fit every city exactly and without exception; both Burgess and Hoyt expected differences to arise, but not enough to upset the fundamental patterns. (Some urban geographers avoid a universal explanation by suggesting that there are subsidiary centres in all cities which exert their own influence and affect the total pattern, breaking down both concentric zones and sectors.) What the two theories have in common is an assumption that the city pattern follows mechanically from growth and decay, and that society moves within the pattern, also mechanically, following changes in functions and in land values. What they fail to take into account is the possibility that society will often give social value to certain sectors irrespective of their real estate value. Idealised patterns break down because of the 'illogical' conservation of values in certain sectors. This means that generalisations even about West European cities must be very few indeed, and that in detail each city is unique. Society and urban environment fit in together but in a way depending greatly on past history and traditions.

9.9 SPHERES OF INFLUENCE

A town cannot live in isolation. The origin of towns lay in the surplus of a countryside which allowed special activities other than growing food. Towns have always lived on the land, and in exchange for their food the people of the countryside expect the specialised services of the townsfolk. The town is therefore the centre of exchange. Town and country depend on one another, and one of the geographer's tasks is to study this relationship and to define the region which is dependent on any one town. There are certain limits to the region within which the urban–rural link is practicable. In medieval Europe market towns were closely spaced, because the limit over which a farmer could be expected to walk to the market–with his livestock–and home again after transacting his business was about 5 km. This meant that markets were only about 9 km apart. In the last couple of hundred years men have become much more mobile, but they are still reluctant to travel too far to a frequent market. The region within which people tend to look to one town is sometimes called the *umland*. This has also been called the *urban field*, a parallel with the magnetic field within which particles are attracted to one particular point. The field can be drawn by measuring the distances of the *pull* of the various services which a town provides. For example, if a town publishes a local newspaper, plotting the local items will show exactly how far afield it is read and has influence. Plotting the districts visited by delivery vans from food stores gives a good indication of the extent of influence of a town, and the distribution of pupils attending a secondary school shows another sphere of influence. Often these influences coincide to give a fairly well-defined region linked in many ways, both economic and social, with the town which is its hub.

One method which has been devised of showing the urban fields of these smaller market towns is by plotting the frequency of bus services into them. There is a point between each town which is rather like a human watershed: on one side people move to town A, on the other to town B, and this is reflected in the frequency of the bus services to those towns.

So far we have been thinking in terms of market towns such as those of England and Wales, which are frequently spaced and which consequently have fairly small urban fields. In addition to the day-to-day needs of its own people, such towns normally provide the weekly market needs of the surrounding area together with places of entertainment, secondary schools, doctors and solicitors. For more occasional needs and for specialist services, people must travel farther to bigger towns; for example, for hospital services, larger and specialised stores, luxury shops, higher education facilities. A town providing these will serve a much larger field, and will itself contain several smaller fields within it. There is, in fact, a hierarchy of towns and of urban fields, from the small market town to the county town, where certain administrative functions are concentrated, to the regional centre and finally to the metropolis. People's needs and movements are geared to this hierarchy in such a way that the frequency of visits decreases as the size of the town increases and as the possible distance away from the town increases. A metropolitan city like London may be called a first-order town because in some spheres such as government, entertainment and luxury goods and specialist facilities, it serves the whole of Britain. On a slightly lower level of services it shares certain functions with second-order towns, like Bristol, Birmingham, Liverpool or Leeds. At this level London serves only the south-east of England, and the other major cities have an equal attraction for people living within their respective fields. Within these again are third-order towns, and so on, down the hierarchy. There is, then, a direct relationship between the size and function of a city and its urban field.

London is usually referred to as a metropolitan city. Such is the importance of urban life in Western Europe and North America, that a country may be dominated by one or many metropolitan cities, all of which can give the largest number of urban services. Metropolitan influence is measured in the same way as the urban field of a market town, but the scale is different. In highly urbanised countries the dominance of metropolitan cities is clearly marked. To some extent and for a greater or less time, possibly periodically, the life of the whole country is tuned towards its greatest cities; and it is from here that goods, services and communications are distributed to the metropolitan regions.

SUGGESTIONS FOR FURTHER READING

R. E. DICKINSON: *City and Region* (Routledge and Kegan Paul), 1965.

A. HAWLEY: *Human Ecology* (Ronald Press), New York, 1950.

H. M. MAYER and C. F. KOHN: *Readings in Urban Geography* (Chicago), 1959.

T. G. McGEE: *The City in South-East Asia* (Bell), 1967.

R. E. MURPHY: *The American City* (McGraw-Hill), 1966.

H. J. NELSON: 'A Service Classification of American Cities' *Economic Geography*, XXXI, 1955.

R. E. PAHL: *Patterns of Urban Life* (Longman), 1970.

G. SJOBERG: *The Pre-industrial City* (Free Press), Illinois, 1960.

A. E. SMAILES: *The Geography of Towns* (Hutchinson), 1960.

A. E. SMAILES: 'The Urban Hierarchy in England and Wales', *Geography*, XXIX, 1944.

A. E. SMAILES: 'Analysis and Delimitation of Urban Fields', *Geography*, XXXII, 1947.

G. A. THEODORSON: *Studies in Human Ecology* (Peterson), 1961.

Chapter 10

COMMUNICATIONS

10.1 ROUTEWAYS

Just as a study of population distribution without consideration of migrations might lead to false conclusions, so settlement
studies are incomplete without the very thing which gives them
life–i.e. communication. Routeways have figured prominently
in history and geography, and roads, railways and ports are all
features of the landscape which demand study, both in their
own right and for the effect which they may have on the distribution of other features. The word communication is used
because all contacts have some relevance to the geographer,
and it is true that telecommunications of all kinds can lead
to culture contacts without movements of men. But the geographer is more concerned with human movements, the means
by which these are effected, and the relationship between the
pattern of movement and other features on the face of the
earth.

The first consideration must be lines of movements, or
routeways (Fig. 10.1). Long before the development of any
kind of transport movements of men were canalised by their
choice of easy gradient rather than steep, by the availability
of water, by the presence of rivers. Thus mountain passes and
river valleys figure prominently from earliest times, and
forested land was avoided. Given the human circumstances –
the need for contact, the compulsion to move, the desire to
expand – major routeways soon become immediately apparent.
Among the very early ones must be counted the 'fertile cres-
cent' between Sumeria and Egypt, delimited by aridity but
itself blessed by water: or the amber route from the Baltic to
the Mediterranean, crossing those great east–west lines of
movement, the Danube valley and north European plain.
During the prehistoric period, too, the north-west fringe of

Europe was being peopled from the sea; sailors who had ventured beyond the Pillars of Hercules clung to the shores of Iberia, France and Brittany before reaching the western promontories of Britain. Here the Irish Sea itself became the route centre of the Celtic cultures, from megalithic times, through the so-called Age of Saints down even to modern times.

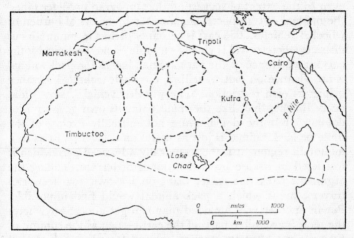

Fig. 10.1. Caravan routes across the Sahara. The main oases are shown by open circles.

Trade was always a great incentive to movement. Europe in medieval times was traversed by merchant routes which linked the great fairs, and caravans crossed the Sahara and central Asia along very well-defined ways where water was the prime consideration. Another incentive was the search for new land. In the early 19th century the United States was crossed by a few well-defined trails along which tens of thousands walked and rode; the Oregon trail and the Santa Fé trail are among the best known.

'Given the human circumstances' is a term which must be stressed. It is human movement which makes the trail; there is a tendency to forget this because we argue from *known* human routeways back to the seemingly 'natural' route. Even the Hudson Mohawk gap was a closed corridor until the Indians of the Mohawk valley had been subdued; it was after this, at the very end of the 18th century, that the gap assumed its modern significance.

Vidal de la Blache emphasises the close relationship between primitive modes of travel and the physical environment, even to the extent of suggesting that topography 'determines' the method of transportation, whether by beasts of burden or wheeled vehicles. The cart is certainly useless in mountainous districts where travel is chiefly on mule back. Technically the cart is an advance on the pack animal, just as the pack animal is an advance on foot travelling, but each technical advance brings its own restriction. 'The wheeled vehicle', says Vidal de la Blache, 'has, like the mule path, its own geographical domain.' But the domains are not mutually exclusive: the mule or pack animal is just as useful on a level plain as in a mountain region—it is the technically advanced cart which is restricted in its use by certain kinds of terrain. Taking the argument back one stage, man, on his own two feet, can traverse areas which a pack animal would find impossible. Put in another way, unaided man can get almost anywhere; the most inaccessible parts of the earth—such as the summit of Everest—can often be reached only on foot; by pack animal man can get *almost* anywhere; by cart he can travel freely only on fairly level natural surfaces—plains, steppes, plateaus. Within this kind of landscape, lines of movements often vary within wide limits, although stopping points, sometimes controlled by water supplies and food depots, are fairly permanent. But once the next stage in communications is introduced —the artificially made road—movement is restricted to very narrow limits; another technical innovation has brought its own limitations. Even so, a well-populated country can be traversed by a close network of roads which are fairly adaptable to sudden physiographic changes: they can take a sharp slope or a sudden curve. The technical requirements of railways restrict the possible lines of movements much more severely, just as sheer cost prohibits a dense network of local lines. The requirements of modern planes are very exacting and suitable bases near large cities are sometimes difficult to find. The number of major airfields is comparatively small. The logical, and almost incredible, conclusion of this progression, both in techniques and in the limitations they impose, was the Bristol Brabazon plane, which had an airfield constructed specially for it; the expense was such that no other comparable field was built. The Brabazon was so demanding that it literally could go nowhere.

The sequence is an interesting one and it has a parallel in water transport. In the days of sailing craft any small port could serve as a port of departure or arrival. For example, in the early 19th century one could have sailed to the New World from any of a score of ports in Wales alone. But the large passenger vessel of the later 19th century could use only the big ports, and Liverpool and Southampton became the established centres of emigration.

10.2 ROADS

Much as a routeway may contribute to the geography of a region, the artificial road is the first permanent man-made feature of the landscape. Paved roads immediately bring to mind the Romans, though the system was known in China long before the Christian era. The Roman achievement was in producing a pattern of roads which primarily served strategic and political purposes. 'All roads lead to Rome' was almost literally true, for the road was a direct link from the centre of the empire to its farthest domain (Fig. 10.2). It was a strategic pattern with an eye mainly to origin and destination, and sometimes hardly deigned to consider the minutiae of topography; it was the work of engineers and soldiers. The Inca civilisation produced a similar system. Theirs, too, was a strategic pattern, linking all parts of their empire by a network dominated by two north–south roads, one coastal, one Andean. The latter, straight as a Roman road, was only a metre wide and often surmounted steeper slopes by series of cut steps, for the Inca, in common with other New World peoples, had no wheeled vehicles.

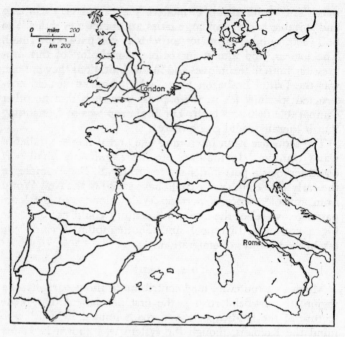

Fig. 10.2. The Roman roads of Europe.

It is interesting to compare the military and strategic road, Roman or medieval or comparatively modern, with local roads, the former concerned with rapid movement in terms of an entire state or empire, the latter serving strictly local needs. Compare the local network in Northern Ireland, lazily avoiding every drumlin, with the Anglo-Norman road which cuts with startling directness from Drumglass into the interior (Fig. 10.3). Compare the network of local roads near a former Roman road in Britain, Watling Street, now the A5. No two systems could be more dissimilar (Fig. 10.4). Watling Street, its prime function forgotten with the decline of Rome, had probably virtually disappeared when the local road system came into being in early medieval times, specifically to link villages, as it still does today. Watling Street became paved only comparatively recently (even today a part of it near the Watford gap is unpaved) to serve newer needs for direct road traffic, for at this point Telford's road to Holyhead ran to the west of it. This explains the lack of villages along this long stretch of the A5. For normally roads attract settlement; in times of peace they are lines of movement and contact. A third pattern has now appeared in the Watford gap area; this

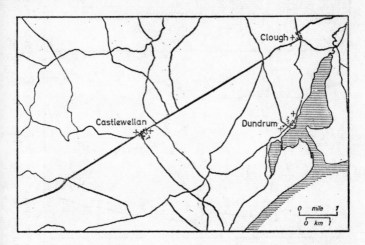

Fig. 10.3. The contrast between a military road and the local network in south Co. Down, Northern Ireland.

is the M1 motorway, specifically adapted to motor transport. This is a superimposed line of communication, not only unrelated to local needs, but deliberately cut off from them. This is a return–though under very different conditions–of the national road, the link between two distant points; and once again, by design, no settlement will be attracted to it. In Europe most of the road network has been inherited from a past age, and it reflects (a) the local network, and (b) the national, strategic, road system linking capital cities with outlying provinces. The trunk roads of Britain are an excellent

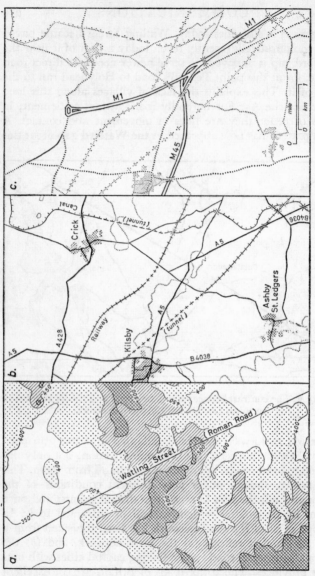

Fig. 10.4. Stages in communication patterns in the Watford gap. The strategic road (*a*) gave way to the local system (*b*) but was re-established by railways and motorways (*c*).

example of the latter, for the links are between London and Edinburgh, Glasgow, Ireland via Holyhead, Ireland via Fishguard and the naval ports of the south and south-east. This most recently inherited system, emphasising the place of the capital city, arose in Great Britain in the early 19th century, when road surfacing was transformed by Macadam and when engineers like Telford tackled major obstacles by new engineering techniques, resulting in such feats as spanning the Menai Straits with a suspension bridge in 1826. The major roads now tended to take on a Roman-like radial pattern at variance with small local networks. It is repeated in many countries. The post-Napoleonic road system of France emphasises clearly the dominance of Paris and the strategic significance of the roads, linking the capital city as they do with Metz, Dijon, Calais and Le Havre, Brest and Bordeaux and with the Mediterranean at Marseilles (Fig. 10.5).

This pattern, so familiar in the Old World, is rarely found in the New. Here the early road systems penetrated the interior as European settlement extended inland. In North America, for example, many of the inland trails became roads – if only, at first, corduroy roads (i.e. sawn trunks laid in a long ribbon, looking rather like a narrow strip of corduroy). Perhaps the most famous of these was the Cumberland road, from Baltimore, through the Cumberland Gap to Wheeling, Indianapolis and eventually to St. Louis. The transcontinental pattern today is that of half a dozen highways linking east and west, often separated from each other by hundreds of miles and with remarkably few crosslinks.

The use of roads has undergone a revolution, both in the nature and number of vehicles using them. It is one of the accepted anomalies of our time that roads intended for horse-drawn vehicles and reflecting either local needs or national, are now used by cars, lorries, buses, bicycles – and pedestrians! With few exceptions 20th-century communication in Britain is fitted into an early 19th-century road system much of which is derived from even earlier times. The response to new demands is piecemeal, yet enough has been done for us to recognise new elements, quite different from the old. Firstly,

P

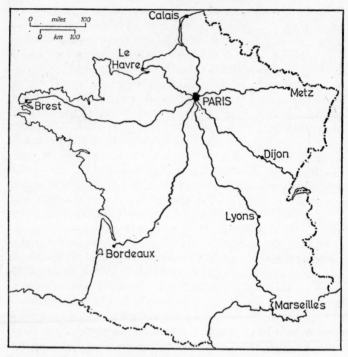

Fig. 10.5. The main post-Napoleonic roads of France were strategic, centring on Paris.

new motorways are restricted to motor vehicles; secondly, they facilitate fast movement; thirdly, to do this, from an engineering viewpoint they resemble railroads, for gradient is carefully controlled and consequently cuttings, embankments and bridges are frequent and curves are very wide. In order to accommodate several lines of traffic in two directions, a wide swathe is cut through the countryside. In Britain this has not yet raised the problem of maintaining a wide level of ribbon of land in uneven and rugged country; in mountain topography the two parts of the road may well have to divide, as in southern Germany. Another characteristic of the motor-

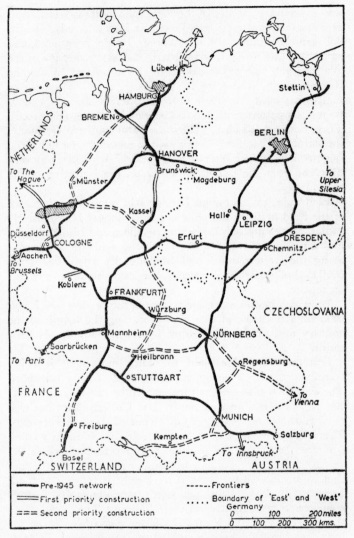

Fig. 10.6. The German autobahnen system.

way is its independence of the local road system, which runs as a quite separate pattern linked at intervals only, and its deliberate avoidance of built-up areas. Its aim is national, and again it is interesting that in Britain the M1 makes use of the Watford gap referred to above in the same way as did the Roman road. Where, as in Germany, a whole system of motorways exist (Autobahnen), the interest lies in the contrast of its pattern with the former radial pattern (Fig. 10.6). These new roads link the North Sea and southern Germany, the Baltic and southern Germany, the east and west industrial regions. It is, in fact, inter-regional and strategic in a way very different from the former emphasis on the centrality of the capital city.

In Britain, too, although London will retain its dominance of the road network the pattern will no longer be exclusively radial. More emphasis is given to northern and Midland links, and a motorway will link the north-east with the south-west along the western border of England. By 1970, 604 miles (966 km) of motorway were complete, and 345 miles (522 km) on tender.

Italy also has an extensive system of motorways which will soon offer a choice of two routes running the length of the country and uniting the industrial north with the extreme south.

Gradually the oldest aid to man's movement is being transformed with a system suited to 20th century transport. The danger is that new motorways will be insufficient to take the great increase in road users. The United States has well over 100 million vehicles, 85 per cent of them private cars. There the problem is most acute inside the cities. In a small country like Britain the pressure is apparent everywhere. Its 12 million cars are a major problem, aggravated by the fact that in Britain 58 per cent of all freight is moved by road. Incidentally some of the new roads have demanded feats of engineering, particularly in bridge-building. The bridges over the Severn, Tay and Forth, the latter 7,000 feet (2,100 m) long, are beautiful monuments to this most recent phase of transportation.

10.3 RAILWAYS

In discussing motorways we have moved from the technical stage of horse-drawn vehicles to that of the motor-car, and in so doing have leap-frogged another stage in transport which has had a great effect on human geography. The railway is certainly an integral part of the British landscape; the steam trail was formerly as familiar as the clouds. The technical demands of the railway, let alone its cost, introduced restrictions on movement. The grading of the permanent way, cuttings, embankments, viaducts and bridges are massive works which have given us some of the greatest landscape modifications made by man, monuments to early Victorian ingenuity and tenacity of purpose. The entire programme reflected the new technology of steam, and the ability to handle iron on a scale unknown before.

The pattern of communications which emerged in the mid-19th century in Europe was not unlike that of the post-road; a radial pattern, primarily strategic, and linking the capital with the farthermost points of the state. In France it duplicated the road pattern, but added lines from Paris to Cherbourg and the Belfort gap. In Britain post-road and rail patterns were almost identical, with the addition of a line to Plymouth. Local lines were much fewer than roads. Material for the new railway lines was rarely local and costs were very high. In this respect it is interesting to compare the pattern of post-roads in Ireland in the 19th century with the railways (Fig. 10.7). The roads linked Dublin directly with nine regional centres at the periphery of the island. The railways consisted of four lines from Dublin which branched as they penetrated the country.

In the new countries, this radial pattern broke down, as it had with roads. There the railroad's job was to penetrate the interior. The towns on the eastern seaboard of the U.S.A. each tried desperately to be the first to tap the interior, and New York's taking advantage of the Hudson Mohawk gap probably made that city what it is today. West of the Mississippi the fairly close pattern typical of the eastern half of the United

States even today thins out to the four transcontinental lines linking east and west.

In the U.S.S.R. Moscow is the centre of a radial network not unlike that of Paris or London, but beyond the Urals are the comparatively new lands of Russia, and the solitary trans-Siberian line takes up its transcontinental task of linking east and west. Until recently this line was single tracked for much of its length. There is a loop around the Aral basin, and in the

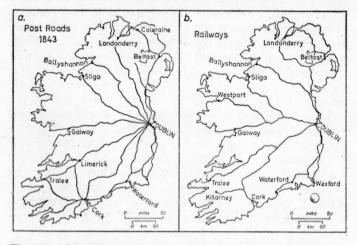

Fig. 10.7. Irish post-roads connected Dublin directly with distant towns (*a*) in contrast with the main railway lines (*b*).

east the Harbin branch was for long an alternative route from Karimskaya.

Railways made movement in the last century very much easier; they led to the concentration of population in capitals and in other cities; they attracted industry; they attracted settlement and they created new towns (like Crewe and Swindon); they aided the development of new countries which depended on the distribution of supplies and goods from the older established centres.

In the older developed countries railways are on the wane:

in the new they are on the increase. The following table shows the relative use of major forms of transporting freight and passengers within certain countries (1965).

	Rail	Water	Road	Pipeline
		(per cent)		
Poland	95	1	4	—
Czechoslovakia	89	—	11	—
Soviet Union	84	6	6	4
Turkey	54	46	*	*
France	52	9	30	9
United States	44	16	23	17
United Kingdom	31	—	68	1
Italy	26	1	72	1

(* no information)

Rail is still the vastly predominant mode of transport in Eastern Europe, but its decline in the United States, United Kingdom and Italy can be related directly to improvements in roads. This is particularly so in Italy and the United Kingdom. In the latter rail linkage has been reduced by nearly a third, but the remainder is being modernised to provide a challenging alternative to roads. Steam disappeared in 1968: diesel and electricity share power. With speeds increasing to more than 100 m.p.h. some intercity lines have shown a dramatic increase in the number of passengers. In the United States the use of rail has been declining for half a century, and passengers have been lost to air transport in particular. In 1968 air passenger miles were more than double those of rail.

Closures of railways in the United States, Britain, France and Germany are balanced by the opening of new lines in under-developed countries and Japan.

One of the most far-reaching technical changes in railway development has been containerisation, i.e. the handling of freight in standard containers, which are carried by direct and fast routes to centres especially equipped to deal with them. 'Freightliners' may well change the balance between the amount of goods carried on road and rail.

10.4 WATER TRANSPORT

It was the industrial revolution which gave birth to the

railway, but for some years it had its work cut out to prove it-self superior to another means of transport which was linked with that revolution–the canal. Before discussing canals something must be said very briefly about the place of water-ways in communications.

Man must have realised the possibilities of river transport at a very early stage of cultural development. In forest en-vironments in particular, the river offered an obvious route–a permanent and known way in otherwise uncharted country, and one which could be used by fairly simple adaptation of logs, or rafts, or by more elaborate canoes and boats. In medieval times and later, Europe's waterways became the framework of commercial life. On them grew and thrived im-portant cities in which the river was the great highway; often it was the processional way as in medieval London, its width contrasting strangely with the narrowness and inconvenience of medieval streets. Today the Thames offers only a limited entry into lowland England, but other European rivers, the Rhine, Seine, Rhone, are greater commercial arteries than ever before. Russia's three immense rivers, the Ob (with its tributary the Irtish), the Yenesei and Lena, although north-ward flowing to the Arctic sea, link the old-established wheat belt, along which runs the trans-Siberian railway, with the less-developed Siberian lands. With greater economic develop-ment in Siberia their role might increase considerably. The fact that they are frozen over in winter is no disadvantage; for in their frozen state they provide almost perfect highways of negligible gradient, along which caterpillar tractor trains are capable of drawing vast loads.

In the new countries rivers were easy points of penetration for exploration, permanent limits to territorial claims, and ready made highways for later settlement. Much of the history of the United States could be written around the Hudson, the Ohio, Mississippi, Missouri and Platte rivers. The Mississippi system linked a whole continent at a time when settlers were only just discovering the new west; and not until east–west routes had crossed half the continent did it lose its supremacy in trade and movement. The great hey-day of its river boats was a mere century ago. To the north the St. Lawrence provided another gateway to the heart of the continent, and together with the traffic of the Great Lakes is now a major commercial routeway.

It was only a step from man's efforts to improve natural waterways, by widening, deepening and scouring, to increase the network of navigable water by building canals. In the rice lands of China canal building is an old art, combining irrigation and water control, but at the same time providing means of communication in closely settled country where land is at a premium: a canal is often a town's High Street. Reclamation and control led to similar close canal networks in Holland. But in Britain we link canal building with the early phases of the industrial revolution. By 1790 lowland Britain was traversed with a complex canal system whose building showed considerable engineering skill, for contour canals were limited in use, and lock systems, tunnels and aqueducts soon showed that a new technical stage was being initiated which overcame many natural obstacles. It was not until the middle of the 19th century that the supremacy of railways was accepted and canals began to be superseded. In the meantime canals were augmenting the river transport systems in Europe, and in the U.S.A. the Erie Canal (1824), linking the Hudson valley with the 'new west', was among the first of many factors which gave New York its commercial supremacy. Canals made navigable the entire St. Lawrence routeway, culminating in the mid-20th century, in the St. Lawrence Waterway.

But canals not only increased internal communications. The canal engineers' skill was also called upon to link the seas. The first of these massive projects was the Caledonian Canal (1822), linking the North Sea and the Atlantic. As a short cut for traffic which otherwise had to round the northern tip of Scotland, this canal was never very successful, though heavy traffic in the First World War underlined its strategic value. Strategy also gave birth to the Kiel Canal, linking the Baltic and the North Sea; strategy also prompted the building of the world's greatest canal links, Suez and Panama, both of which have had a marked effect on world transport routes

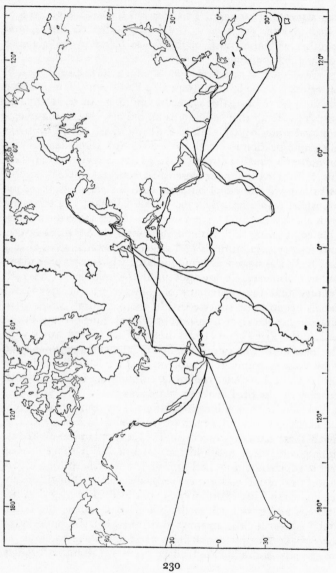

Fig. 10.8. Major shipping routes show the importance of the major canals.

(Fig. 10.8). The former, built in 1869, links four inland lakes, is 137 km/85 miles long, but has no locks. The latter, opened in 1914, called for extraordinary engineering skill and perseverance: it ascends 26 m/85 feet, descends 10 m/31 feet and has three double locks; but it saves 7,900 miles in a voyage from New York to San Francisco.

The effect of the two great canals on major world routes was immense. In 1966 Suez handled 274 million tons of shipping and Panama 100 million tons. They formed two of the four great nodes of sea movement where transport concentrated. All Atlantic–Pacific movement came together at Panama, and Suez was the node for the vast bulk of traffic from the Atlantic and Europe to the east and Australia. (The other two nodes are the English Channel, connecting northern and central Europe with the Atlantic, and Singapore.) Suez was blocked by the United Arab Republic in 1967 and is still unusable, and this has meant a reversal of routes of almost exactly a century: ships to the east must again take the Cape route.

These canals are among the final stages of sea communication, for man's adaptation to sea travel has a long history. The challenge of the sea, a totally different environment demanding such specialist adaptation, has been met by comparatively few societies. Its conquest, as Vidal de la Blache says, is 'the privilege of small groups'. It is probable that man first ventured on the sea in order to get food, that the familiarity which this brought led to commerce and thereby established links between all seaboard communities. The degree to which men have been able to master the new medium has depended – as on land – on a series of innovations, some of which belong to remote antiquity. The ability to construct a stable vessel, the invention of oars, of the rudder, and of sails, were all major advances. The last utilised natural energy in the form of wind-power, and so this to some extent determined men's routeways. The alternating winds of Monsoon Asia, the seasonal winds of the Mediterranean, all led to cultural links, to the diffusion of ideas, and to the spread of commerce. Later techniques enabled men to use the wind more subtly to determine a vessel's course. Most early sailing was coastal, or point to point, until the invention of the compass and its adoption in Europe. But however great the technical modifications, the sailing ship was ultimately dependent on the world's great wind belts. The peak of sailing achievement is as recent as the 1860's, when the famous New England clippers made very fast time indeed. The *Flying Cloud* made the journey from New York to San Francisco in 89 days, an average of 365 km/227 miles a day over 26 days; in one day it recorded 602 km/374 miles. But the peak of sailing also saw the beginning of the mastery of steam, and this had several radical effects on sea communications. Firstly, the steam vessel was not dependent on wind belts. Secondly, the size of vessels increased enormously, and very quickly: the *Great Western* registered 20,000 tons, the *Queens* are over 80,000 tons. Thirdly, time was saved and movements became regular: a sailing vessel took an indeterminate time, but even the earliest steamships could sail and arrive to strict schedule. By 1864 the Atlantic was being crossed in 12½ days, by 1891 in 7½, which is not appreciably greater than the average Atlantic crossing of today.

But the mid-twentieth century saw further developments in the size and function of vessels. Whereas the giant passenger liners, in face of air competition, survive only as prestige symbols, freight-carrying demands ever larger and more specialised vessels. The most spectacular are oil tankers. By 1970 there were over 40 tankers with a deadweight (i.e. the weight of cargo they can carry) of over 213,000 tons: all were over 1,000 feet long. Increase in size and speed and a switch to diesel power, and construction for specific purposes are rapidly changing merchant fleets. The multicargo vessel is on the way out: the tanker, ore-carrier, wine vessel, container ship, are taking over.

Container ships are the counterpart of the railways freight-liner, goods being packed in standard containers. This has revolutionised cargo handling and the speed of transfer of goods, and it has also meant a radical change in the design of ports. Ports and harbours have to keep pace with changing technology and are consequently becoming even more specialised. Tilbury, on the Thames, has been extensively replanned. Six of its 13 deep water berths are designed for container handling, and it is also a freightliner terminus. Seaforth, on the Mersey, is the newest container port to become operative, but there are also container facilities at Harwich, Greenock, Felixstowe, Manchester, Newport and Grangemouth. Port Talbot and Immingham are specialised ore terminals. Immingham is also designed to handle tankers, but the specialised oil terminals of Britain are Isle of Grain (Thames), Liverpool, Milford Haven, Fawley and Finnant (Clyde). Previously most docks handled a variety of goods, though there was some specialisation, such as passenger traffic at Liverpool and Southampton, packet boats at Dover and naval vessels at Portsmouth.

From the beginning the steam vessel had one disadvantage compared with the sailing vessel: it had to carry its own fuel, and on longer routes this meant the need for refuelling bases, many of which also became repair and cleaning depots. Like caravanserai in the desert, these are very often tiny islands across which the route passes. The strategic significance of many of these routes emphasises the need for these bases. When naval power was at its height the British Empire, for example, depended on its bases at Gibraltar, Malta, Cyprus, Aden and Singapore to protect the route from Britain to Australasia. American dominance in the Pacific depends upon the use of Hawaii, Midway, Wake, Anam, Pago Pago and the Aleutians.

10.5 AIR TRANSPORT

It is only in this century, and for practical purposes only since the 1920's, that the third element has been conquered and the air opened to communications. First thoughts may suggest that this development has introduced an element of freedom never experienced before, because theoretically there are no barriers to flight between any two points on the earth's surface. This is not strictly true, but nevertheless some basically new possibilities and considerations arise. Air transport is very flexible; it need not recognise the difference between land and

water masses–and consequently, there need be no tranship-
ment between one continental city and another; it is speedy;
and it requires neither roads nor tracks. The potential use of
great circle routes has introduced a new look in world communications maps. The Mercator, in many ways so suited to
showing routes, is now outdated; Zenithal Equidistant and
Gnomonic projections are more suitable for the air age, but
new projections are also being invented specifically to show
world airways (Fig. 10.9).

Although an ideal pattern of communications can be constructed on the basis of linking major population centres, the
actual pattern of air routes does not strictly fit into it. The most
dense cluster of routes are (a) within the United States,
(b) within Europe and the Mediterranean, and (c) linking
Europe and the United States. There are lesser clusters linking Europe with South America, South Africa and south-east
Asia. Most routes link not only areas of high population, but
those with a high standard of living.

Much of the traffic in the air is international and deals with
passengers rather than with freight. City to city services are
relatively new in Britain, though in the United States the
scale of intercity services becomes international. In 1969 air-
lines in Britain dealt with nearly 30 million passengers: 14·3
million used London's major airport at Heathrow, though
11·3 million of these were on international flights: Gatwick,
also serving London, handled 3 million passengers in 1969.

Of the physical difficulties encountered in flying, major
mountain ranges are still significant. Although height is no
barrier, mountains affect air currents and weather, thus introducing a new hazard: they also lack emergency landing areas.
The Himalayan–Pamir–Nan Shan ranges in Asia separate
the Europe to south-east Asian routes from the central Asian
quite effectively; though this merely confirms a fundamental
divide in human movement, and there is no demand yet for
cross routes. But the greatest physical hazard is weather.
Temperature, pressure, cloud amount and formation, fog and
icing are all vital factors, and equally important are wind
force and direction. The winds in the upper atmosphere are

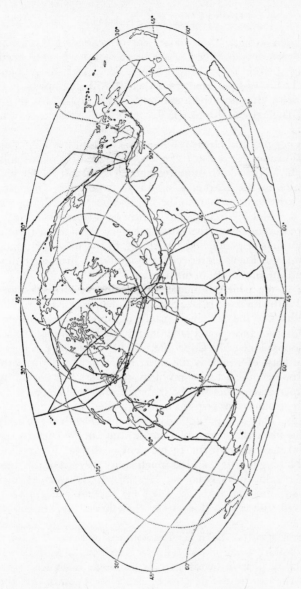

Fig. 10.9. The Nordic projection is specially designed to show major air routes.

very much stronger than those near the earth's surface, and their direction is different. Much more data needs to be accumulated before some of these meteorological phenomena are fully understood, and even then it will be impossible to make allowance for them all or for the rapid changes in meteorological conditions which are difficult to forecast accurately.

One last physical element limits the apparent freedom of air communications and that is the location and siting of airfields. These have their own requirements of size, a level terrain, proximity to the market and safety. Needs vary from the simple airstrip or airfield to the large airport with all the terminal facilities for freight and passenger carrying. The technical requirements of the latter are very considerable, from the handling of goods and passengers to the need for taking the largest airliner; moreover there should be little air pollution and the minimum of obstruction.

One factor which is making the siting of airfields more critical is the increase in size and speed of airliners. The Jumbo Jet, with twice the carrying capacity of large planes, demands long runways and special facilities for fast handling of traffic. Supersonic planes, like Concorde, will bring special problems, not the least of which is the sonic boom in the flight path. Noise has become a major problem, and there is a possibility that supersonic planes will be banned from some airports. To meet these objections airports tend to be sited away from built-up areas. This is a paradoxical situation. Heathrow is only 14 miles from the centre of London, but the journey to the terminal may account for 13 per cent of the total travelling time of a long journey, and as much as 40 per cent of the time of a short journey. Even so, Heathrow's six square miles (15·54 sq kms) and 9,500 ft (2,898 m) runway are minimal. A second runway will soon be lengthened to 12,800 ft (3,900 m).

These difficulties have been epitomised in the search for a site for a third London airport. Fast transport links and good accessibility give little margin for an obvious choice. Ultimately the case rested on environmental arguments, and the site at Foulness was the one which least disturbed the life of the countryside and of its people.

It is difficult to forecast whether better links will diminish the inconvenience of outlying airports or whether major technical improvements in aircraft design will enable airports to be built nearer city centres. Certainly the problems of siting are vital if the airliner's greatest asset–that of providing direct links–is to be maintained.

SUGGESTIONS FOR FURTHER READING

J. H. APPLETON: *A Geography of Communications in Great Britain* (Oxford University Press), 1962.

C. HADFIELD: *British Canals* (Phoenix House), 1950.

A. C. O'DELL: *Railways and Geography* (Hutchinson), 1956.

K. R. SEALY: *The Geography of Air Transport* (Hutchinson), 1957.

INDEX

Where a topic appears on more than one page, the principal reference (if any) is indicated in **bold** type.   Figure references are given in *italic* type.